Wicked
MYRTLE BEACH &
the GRAND STRAND

Wicked Myrtle Beach & *the* Grand Strand

Becky Billingsley

THE
History
PRESS

Published by The History Press
Charleston, SC 29403
www.historypress.net

Front cover, map: Library of Congress.

First published 2015

Manufactured in the United States

ISBN 978.1.62619.805.0

Library of Congress Control Number: 2015939774

For the late Horace Carter: Your courage is inspiring.

And for Ann Vereen, Dr. Julie S. von Frank and Ellen Walsh: Thank you for trusting me to research and share your family's tragedy. I'm glad your questions were answered, and may Ellen Connor and the Cullipher family rest in peace.

CONTENTS

ACKNOWLEDGEMENTS

Revealing less than flattering stories about friends, family and yourself isn't easy. Many thanks to those who did for this book in the name of setting the record straight and sharing a history that puts a realistic perspective on our past.

INTRODUCTION

Bootlegging, bordellos, hit-and-run drivers, gambling, slavery, racial segregation and other questionable behavior constitute a significant part of Grand Strand history, and it's a history often ignored, overlooked or sanitized in some historic accounts.

It's natural to want to cast your ancestors in the best possible light, and it's true that many, if not most, of the people who first populated Horry and Georgetown Counties made positive contributions to society. But recording only the good deeds without including the darker incidents, or glossing over them without elaboration, gives an incomplete picture of the Myrtle Beach area's evolution and does a disservice to anyone seeking a well-rounded history. *Wicked Myrtle Beach and the Grand Strand* fills in gaps with accounts native residents might talk about among themselves but don't necessarily write down for others to know.

During the past couple of decades while researching other articles and books, I tucked away remarkable vintage newspaper clippings and made notes of offbeat stories. Many of them are in this book, along with personal interviews conducted with native residents.

In a few cases, those locals didn't want their real names printed—you'll understand why when you read what they had to say—and those people are indicated on first reference and in the bibliography with asterisks by their names. They are real people. I have audio recordings of their interviews.

While Caucasian people often say there have never been and are not currently any race relation problems in the Myrtle Beach area, African

Americans and other minorities, such as Native Americans, usually have different perspectives. Some people are surprised to learn (while others aren't surprised at all) that the KKK was extremely active here in the early 1950s and held rallies and parades for several more decades.

Public proclamations in favor of segregation were normal around here before integration, and that is reflected in the language used in newspapers. In this book, you'll see quotations from articles that refer to African Americans as "Negroes" and "Colored." That's the way it was, and that's the way I've left it when I've used direct quotations. While some might say using such terms wasn't wicked because everyone did it, others say it stung, and it stung all the worse because everyone did it.

Sometimes truth depends on which historic corner you're peering around.

Chapter 1

THE SWING BRIDGE TRAGEDY

About 11:00 p.m. on August 28, 1923, three carloads of friends and family packed up to drive the fifteen miles home to Conway after a fun Tuesday of seeing the sights at Myrtle Beach. A fifteen-year-old named Roberta Connor got out of her parents' vehicle, which was the third car in the line, and climbed into the first car so she could ride with friends.

An hour later, many people in Conway were awakened by wind that carried rain into their homes, and they got up to shut their windows. A few minutes after that, just past midnight, the whistle at the Conway Light and Ice Company began to blow. Usually, "it was blown as a fire alarm, a signal to call workmen and to usher in the New Year," according to an article by Evelyn Snider in the *Independent Republic Quarterly*.

This time, the whistle meant something else.

TREACHEROUS DRIVING

In 1923, cars were new, and roads were narrow and rutted. In many places, the roads those cars traveled that summer night weren't wide enough for one car to pass another on dry and sunny days, much less on rainy nights. Canals and swamps lined the roads, and ditches filled quickly in wet weather. Thunderstorms and heavy showers are common along the South Carolina coast in August.

As the little three-car caravan trundled carefully along at speeds likely not exceeding twenty or thirty miles per hour, their autos were spaced several minutes apart. There was no need to try to keep up with one another because their day in the sun was done and everyone was thinking about home and bed and the next day's chores.

The first car in the line, the one in which Roberta Connor rode with her young friends, reached the Connors' home in Conway without incident. The ride home took about an hour.

The second car had a young man named Willie Cullipher at the wheel, driving his brother's (Sutton Cullipher) used Dort. In the front seat with him was Kitty Belle Norman and Sutton's daughter Ella. In the back seat were Sutton; his wife, Cornelia; and two more Cullipher children.

Julius Sutton Cullipher and Cornelia Anna Price Cullipher were thirty and thirty-seven years old, respectively, on August 28, 1923. Their three children included two girls, ages seven (Hettie) and five (Ella), and a little boy named for his father (Julius G.). He was still a lap baby at age two and a half because he hadn't yet been dethroned. Cornelia came from the Aynor area, and she and Sutton lived there after marrying. Around 1918, the family moved when he took a job at Conway Lumber Company, and they attended the Second Baptist Church of Conway.

The Culliphers went to Myrtle Beach that day to see what was new. It was their first glimpse of the ocean that year.

In the third and final car were Marvin Connor, age sixty-two; his fifty-year-old wife, Cora Ellen Moore Connor; and friends named Mrs. E.G. Norman (Kitty's mother) and Kever Owens. Marvin was a farmer, and he and Ellen had seven children. All were grown and on their own except for fifteen-year-old Roberta.

A Ford touring car with one headlight and one taillight burned out passed Marvin Connor's car. A few miles farther west, the Ford approached the Cullipher car. They were about a half-mile from the steel truss swing bridge that crossed the Waccamaw River and fed into the Conway business district.

The Ford's driver pulled closer. Willie Cullipher got as far to the right as he felt was safe, and the one-eyed Ford swung out to pass at what Willie Cullipher judged was as fast as the car could go, which in those days was likely about forty miles per hour. The road at that spot was particularly narrow; Willie Cullipher later said he intended to pull to the side and let the Ford pass as soon as there was a safe spot to do so.

But the Ford driver passed before Willie could get over. As the Ford and the Cullipher car drew even with each other, the right front wheel

Marvin and Ellen Connor pose with their youngest child, Roberta, who was fifteen years old when her mother drowned in the Waccamaw River. *Ellen Walsh collection.*

area of the Ford hit the Culliphers' left front wheel and fender hard enough to jerk the steering wheel out of Willie's hands. The Culliphers' vehicle was knocked into the ditch, where it tipped and landed on the passenger side.

"Get out of the road!" the Ford driver yelled at Willie.

The Ford slowed down after the impact, and a man stepped out of the car, Willie Cullipher remembered. He saw the car was "full" of people: three men at least and maybe a woman, too. Willie said the driver appeared to be under the influence of liquor.

No one was injured except Sutton Cullipher, who had recently had several operations for appendicitis. His incision was ripped open, and later, the coroner said his wounds were mortal.

Sutton screamed in pain, and Willie told his brother to hush. He said, loud enough for the Ford occupants to hear, that he'd get the Ford's license plate number and report the driver to the law.

The person who stepped out of the car hurriedly got back in, and the Ford left at a high rate of speed, heading toward the bridge that was a half mile away.

About fifteen minutes later, Marvin Connor approached the spot where his friends' car lay on its side in the ditch, and it started to rain hard. Willie Cullipher waved at him to stop.

"They stopped me and said that Cullifer [*sic*] was about dead," Connor testified the next day in a sworn inquest, "and wanted me to take him in my car and carry him to the doctor and I got him in my car and his wife and his three children and my wife, I came with them to the steel bridge."

In the front seat with Marvin Connor was his wife, Ellen. The entire Cullipher family—Sutton; Cornelia; and their children, Hettie, Ella and Julius—were in the back seat. Sutton continued to moan and said he "felt all broken up on the inside and he believed he was killed."

The four other occupants from the Cullipher and Connor vehicles—Kitty Belle Norman and her mother, Kever Owens and Willie Cullipher—began walking toward Conway and toward the bridge.

Two weeks later, Marvin Connor testified under oath about what happened next.

When I started, the road seemed to be very rough and Mr. Cullipher, the wounded man, said, "My God, I can't stand it." Then I drove about as slow as possible, so as not to hurt him any more than was necessary. Then I kept on driving about that rate until I got to the bridge, and when I got to the bridge, I put my foot on the gas feed and shoved the gas to it and ran right up there—the windshield was wet, with rain water, the rain was pouring down and I couldn't see good, and I was not expecting the bridge to be open, I was not studying about it, and I was naturally on it before I knew. The wind was not blowing any that I know of, but the rain was pouring down…I remember this: that it didn't rain hard enough for me to have the curtains up and didn't rain hard enough to blow under there and wet me.

The swing-through truss steel bridge where the Connor car plunged into the Waccamaw River in 1923 was located about a third of a mile upstream from the current Main Street Bridge. *Horry County Museum, Conway, South Carolina.*

The span was "slam open," Connor said, and although he said he was driving only about five miles per hour, the Connors' Dort touring car plunged almost twenty feet into the Waccamaw River.

Only Marvin Connor emerged.

The Dorts

The last two cars in the little caravan were a brand called Dorts. Both Marvin Connor and Willie Cullipher were driving one.

Dorts were made for nine years, from 1915 to 1924, and they were built by the Dort Motor Car Company in Flint, Michigan. Josiah Dort, who became a millionaire from selling horse-drawn carriages, was the founder.

Dort automobiles were manufactured in Flint, Michigan, from 1915 to 1924. Two Dorts were involved in the 1923 Conway bridge tragedy. *Author's collection.*

"Quality Goes Clear Through," an advertisement dated August 1922 says. "New prices of $1095 for the Dort Yale Sedan and $1045 for the Dort Yale Coupe emphasize more than ever their great value. And the widespread demand for these cars, which this year has been largely responsible for an increase of 319 per cent in closed car production, assumes even larger proportions."

The Dort Motor Company was in business until 1924, a year after Josiah Dort's death.

It's hard to say the year of manufacture of the Dorts that Willie Cullipher and Marvin Connor were driving, but the Connors' Dort was described as "old." By 1923, Dorts had been manufactured long enough that they could have been purchased secondhand, which, according to Marvin Connor's descendants, was more plausible than to imagine he bought a brand-new one. Ellen Walsh, Marvin Connor's great-granddaughter, wondered how they afforded a Dort car with curtains all around it. She was under the impression they were poor.

"Their children had to work to make ends meet," Walsh said in 2014, "and then they had a car such as that."

The Connors' Dort was found to have faulty brakes, as a September 6, 1923 article notes:

THE Dort Six has been received with such whole-hearted enthusiasm everywhere that the public response to this remarkable new car can be interpreted as nothing less than national approval. Everywhere there is the same unanimous praise and admiration for its graceful new body lines and powerful new motor and the same prevailing opinion that Dort *has* cut straight through accepted values and established an entirely new standard for six-cylinder motor cars.

The Dort Six Touring Car, $990. The New Dort Six 45-horsepower motor, which is one of the finest pieces of motor design ever conceived, has brought to motorists a new conception of power and flexibility— 2 to 60 miles an hour in high gear; pick-up from 5 to 25 miles in less than nine seconds; 24 miles to the gallon at a speed of 30 miles an hour.

Dort Motor Car Company, Flint

A Complete Line of Six-Cylinder and Four-Cylinder Models

Dort Six-Cylinder Cars, $990 to $1495; at Flint
Dort Four-Cylinder Cars, $865 to $1370; at Flint

DORT SIX HARVARD SEDAN, $1495
(Spare tire extra)

A Dort Six Harvard Sedan was in the six-cylinder line that sold for $990 to $1,495 in 1922. This ad appeared in the *Saturday Evening Post* on December 2, 1922. *Author's collection.*

The road department was interested in finding out if the Dort car which plunged through the open draw bridge last week resulting in the deaths of six people at one time, was in good repair as to brakes.

The car was removed from the river on Thursday and a careful examination of the car was made. The report was that this car was practically without brakes. The bands had become worn and had not been renewed. They would not take hold when the lever was applied for more than about two inches of the circumference of the drum round which they were supposed to work.

It is believed that if the brakes had been in good condition that the car would have been stopped before it went over into the river.

Sutton Cullipher's Dort was purchased used, and the day after the wreck, a man named Harrelson retrieved it from the ditch and took it to Conway. He was the Dort's previous owner and still held a mortgage against it.

PROSPERITY AND RELATED PROBLEMS

In 1923, the population of Horry County was growing steadily for several reasons.

In 1900, a train took passengers from Conway to Myrtle Beach for the first time, bringing an increase of beach tourists. Automobiles were soon being driven around Horry County roads, and from 1922 to 1923, vehicles registered in South Carolina increased by 34 percent, from 95,978 to 128,656.

A swing "through truss" bridge completed in 1912 allowed cars to travel freely between Conway and Myrtle Beach via Socastee. The one-lane bridge, located about a third of a mile north of the Waccamaw River Memorial Bridge that's still in use, was tended day and night and opened to allow tall boats to sail through. When the span was closed, it was chained to prevent it from accidentally swinging open.

World War I was over, the Great Depression was still years away and Horry County thrummed with business activities, from tourism to farming. In 1923, almost five thousand farms produced more than $9 million in crops, with tobacco representing a majority of that money.

Horry County remained drastically segregated in 1923. A new silent movie sweeping the nation and scheduled to be shown on September 11, 1923, at Conway's Pastime Theater was D.W. Griffith's *Birth of a Nation*. It is about a southern family's experiences during the Civil War and how the Ku Klux Klan helped save them from renegade former slaves. The movie spurred a huge KKK membership enrollment in South Carolina and across the United States.

On September 18, 1923, Horry County had its first Ku Klux Klan parade, as far as was known by the editor of the *Horry Herald*. The parade was at 9:00 p.m. in Conway and lasted less than an hour. "The members were in cars," the article says. "The car in front bore the firey [*sic*] cross, one of the emblems of the order, while the other cars to the number of about twenty were full of white robed figures."

Prohibition (1919–33) was the law of the land. But if you didn't brew your own corn liquor, beer or wine or buy from moonshiners or rumrunners and still wanted to catch an alcoholic buzz, you could buy patent medicines. Many tonics and bitters sold in drugstores and in the backs of magazines often contained up to 40 percent alcohol.

AFTER THE PLUNGE

Marvin Connor testified on September 11 that everyone in his Dort screamed as the car tumbled into the river and sank to the bottom. Willie Cullipher said he heard the car fall, and he and the other walkers started running toward the bridge. When they saw what had happened, they began yelling for help.

The *Horry Herald* reported that Connor "scrambled until he was outside and clear of the car and struggled to the surface and swam out behind the clump of bushes south of the bridge head. He could not aid the others in any way."

The first person Marvin Connor remembers seeing on land was Perry Quattlebaum, who had been the bridge tender for about five years and worked at the Conway Light and Ice Co. located near the bridge on the river's west bank—the Conway side.

This tie owned by Marvin Connor was made by his wife, Ellen Connor. *Author's collection.*

A short time after midnight, Quattlebaum heard the fire whistle. He was "packing ice on the back platform and a negro ran up there and said something about what happened on the other side of the bridge. I didn't know until we got there that there was someone overboard. He said a car had run off the bridge or something and I went running. He told me after we got across the bridge near the plant that the bridge was open and I told him it was not. He said, 'Yes it was.' I said, 'There is no boat going through it.' He said, 'It is open.'"

Quattlebaum straightened the bridge and noticed the safety chain was hanging down, loose and free from its normal knots that held the bridge in place for automobile traffic. When he reached the east bank, Quattlebaum saw Marvin Connor, who told him what had happened. J.A. Holt, a Conway police officer, soon arrived. When Connor told Officer Holt about the one-eyed Ford that wrecked the Culliphers' car, Holt immediately thought of Winston Russ, a young man he saw driving over the swing bridge just before midnight. The policeman left the bridge to find Russ.

Ellen Connor (left) posed for this photograph with Elizabeth Snowden before Ellen's death at age fifty in 1923. *Ellen Walsh collection.*

By then, many people had arrived to help, and "after swinging the car up to near the surface of the water, all of the unfortunate people were taken out of the water by daylight on Wednesday morning, except Mrs. Marvin Connor." They dragged the river all day Wednesday, but she remained missing.

The Cullipher family's bodies "were taken to the undertaking establishment of the Kingston Furniture Co. as fast as they were recovered from the water." Coroner L.W. Cooper

The Horry Herald.

CONWAY, S. C., THURSDAY, SEPTEMBER 6, 1923

CONNER DISPUTES THAT HE JUMPED

It appears to be a mistake that Marvin Conner either jumped out of his car, or that he even tried to jump as his car approached the open draw. It was published the none of the newspapers to the effect that he left the car before it went over and thus saved himself. Mr. Conner denies this and says that he had no time to jump, and that he did not think of jumping under the circumstances.

He says that he kept his presence of mind all the way through; that he remembers the noise the car made when it struck the water; that he remembers when he was in the car at the bottom of the river and decided that he would come out and up if it were possible.

BODIES OF FIVE GO TO NICHOLS

Home of Mrs Cullipher Daughter of Gilbert Price

ALL CHURCH MEMBERS

Family Relations and Friends Notified and They Attend Funerals

Following the inquest last Wednesday, the bodies of J. Sutton Cullifer, his wife who was Miss Price, of Nichols, S. C., and the three young children of the two, all drowned at one time when the car of Marvin Conner plunged into the open drawbridge, were taken to Nichols, S. C., for burial.

Mrs. Cullifer was the daughter of Gilbert Price of Nichols. Mrs. Culliffer's brothers and other family relations were notified of her death and they attended the interment and funeral exercises at Nichols. Mr. Culliffer came from Aynor, S. C., where he lived for several years following his marriage. Several years ago he accepted a position with the Conway Lumber Company and held a position with that company at the time of his death. The entire Culliffer family were members of the Second Baptist church of Conway. Their pastor is Rev. J. H. Causey, of Loris R. F. D. No. 1. He was notified as soon as possible but the word did not get to him in time for him to attend their last funeral rites.

The Culliffer family were members of a party of church members made up on last week to visit Myrtle Beach on a day's outing. They had not been to the beach this year. They wanted to to the beach this year.

JIM WILSON IS IN FORD WRECK

Front Wheels Demolished and Windshield Broken Into Fragments

Jim Wilson, a colored employee of the Conway Light & Ice Company, wrecked a Ford car just beyond the Kingston Lake drawbridge, last Sunday afternoon, while driving along at an evidently high rate of speed.

The Ford is said to belong to Archie Wilson to come into Conway to get dinner, perhaps while he was off duty at the plant.

It was a bad wreck. The car showed by the tracks of the wheels that it left the middle of the road and the left front and rear wheels ran down the embankment while the efforts of the driver to keep it in the road or to turn back into the road kept the right hand wheels sliding running along the highway of the fill.

It appeared as if the driver made a last effort to turn it back into the road but the incline was too much and it went over on its side, the rear end sliding back in the bushes against a big stump. The front end stopped over another stump just low enough to catch underneath the steering wheel, and it is a mystery how the driver escaped without serious injury.

The wind shield was broken into fragments, the steering column was bent out of shape. One of the rear wheels was denuded of the rim and only the stubs of what had been spokes remained to show that this fragment had once been a wheel. The tire with the inner tube coming out was thrown off on the way down the embankment. It was said that another party was a passenger in the machine at the time of the accident, but the name of this other party was not obtained.

MANY TRACTS CHANGE HANDS

When Clerk and Sheriff Auctions Come off Monday

BIDDING QUITE LIVELY

One of The Largest Crowds of The Year Attend Sales

Last Monday was legal salesday in Conway. This helped to add to the big crowd that was here anyway attending the tobacco sales on all three of the independent warehouse floors, and delivering to the cooperative warehouses. When the sales were called in front

MRS. CONNER'S BODY IS FOUND

More Than a Mile From Where The Car Plunged Over

The body of Mrs. Cora Ellen Conner, wife of Marvin Conner, one of the unfortunate people who went down to the bottom of the Waccamaw River when the car driven by Marvin Conner, plunged through the open draw at the steel bridges was found by D. M. Watts, captain of one of the river boats, as the boat was passing along the river last Thursday afternoon.

Word of the discovery was brought to the town by Charley Johnson, a colored man. This was about 3:30 o'clock Thursday. A crowd of people gathered as her remains were detached and lifted from the branches of an oak where it had lodged by the edge of the stream, down in the long bend below the place where the car took the plunge. It was believed that the body had floated down the river even further than the place where it was found, as the tide was running up the river at the time and there was an indication that the floating body had been caught up in the branches as it was floating back with this tide.

The remains of Mrs. Conner were removed by the undertaking establishment to the home north of Conway. Coroner L. W. Cooper summoned the jury of inquest to make enquiry again as to the cause of death. The same members of the jury as first empaneled met: C. R. Scarborough, H. E. Cagle, J. W. Taylor, S. P. Hawes, D. F. Sawyer and S. F. Gasque.

The sons and daughters of the deceased had been notified of her death. She is survived by her husband and the following named children: Julian Causey of Columbia; Mrs. C. R. Sessions, whose husband is section master on the Atlantic Coast Line Railway and resides in Marion; Mrs. Etta Selleys, Conway; Mrs J. R. Dew, Raleigh; Miss Roberta Conner, Conway; G. M. Conner, Louisville, Ky., and J. F. Conner of Conway.

She was a member of the Second Baptist church. Her pastor, the Rev. J. H. Causey of Loris, R. F. D. No. 1, was notified of her death in the waters of the river. He was here when her remains were found and removed to the home, where the inquest was held. Her funeral services were held on Friday at 10 o'clock attended by a large circle of kinspeople and loving friends. The interment was at Juniper Bay cemetery near Cedar Grove, about eight miles from Conway. The funeral services were conducted by her pastor.

Men spent four weary days of hard work trying to locate the position of Mrs. Conner's body in the channel of the river. It is now thought that efforts made in removing the other un-

MAKES GOOD SALE ON HIS TOBACCO

Charles L. Turner made a good sale on the tobacco market last week, August 31st, when he disposed of various lots of his crop totaling 600 pounds in all for the total sum of $190.74, thus making an average price of over thirty-one cents.

He lives on the R. F. D. No. 1, Galivants Ferry, and seems to have land very suitable to raising tobacco. An account of sales made from his place and that of his brother and father has appeared in the Herald before.

He attributes what success he has attained to the careful attention he gives the crop from the time of planting to the time of placing it on the market. The highest price last Friday realized by him was 35c, and the lowest 8c.

REPORT FINDS FOR THE BANK

W. L. Bryan, Special Referee Decides For Bank of Aynor

DEFENSE MAKES APPEAL

Case Concerns a Mortgage Covering Brick Building in Conway

Among the cases recently tried in the referee court is that of Bank of Aynor against W. C. Adams, for the foreclosure of a mortgage of real estate. An account of the hearing appeared in the Horry Herald about two months ago.

Under an order of judge W. H. Townsend the case was referred to W. L. Bryan, Clerk of the Court as special referee, to take the testimony and report the same to the court together with his conclusions of both law and fact.

The mortgage secured a debt of $10,500.00 and was renewed once after it was first given and after the giving of the renewal there was a payment made on the debt of $3,000.00.

The suit was brought early this year to foreclose and the defendant answered the complaint claiming that he had paid too high a rate of interest, or what was in effect about that same thing, that he had been charged an amount over and above the rate of eight per cent.

The plaintiff replied to the claim of usury setting up that the defendant had agreed to pay a part or all of the loss that would be sustained by the bank upon selling over ten thousand dollars worth of liberty bonds at less

The body of Cora Ellen Connor was found on August 30, 1923, more than a mile downriver from the bridge her car plunged from on August 28. *Horry County Library, Conway, South Carolina.*

determined the children died from drowning because there were no other obvious injuries to their bodies. The children were found inside the Dort with their mother. Sutton Culliper's body was outside the car.

The Cullipers' car was removed from the ditch on Wednesday, August 29. The Connors' car remained in the river until Thursday, August 30, "when it was towed down to the landing at the wharves here and it was there removed," the *Horry Herald* reported on September 6. "It had sustained some damage."

Also on Thursday afternoon, Cora Ellen Connor's body "was found by D.M. Watts, captain of one of the river boats…A crowd of people gathered as her remains were detached and lifted from the branches of an oak where it had lodged by the edge of the stream, down in the long bend below the property of the Conway Lumber Company. This was more than a mile from the place where the car took the plunge."

Ellen Walsh says her grandmother, who was Ellen Connor's daughter, told her that flowers from her hat helped direct searchers to her body. "She had been wearing a large brim hat covered in flowers…She said there were

Ellen Connor was skilled with needles and made fanciful tatted creations like this miniature purse. *Author's collection.*

Ellen Connor's grave is at Juniper Bay Baptist Church cemetery near Conway. The inscription reads, "She was a kind affectionate wife a fond mother and a friend to all." *Author's collection.*

flowers floating downstream from where the body was hung up in the water, and that was one thing that made them take notice that she was somewhere near. What a sad sight it had to be."

Ellen Connor's body was "removed by the undertaking establishment to the home north of Conway," and the next day, Friday, August 31, her funeral was held.

Wind or Whim

Conway residents burned with questions. Who was in the Ford with one headlight? Was it Winston Russ? Was it bootleggers? Did the driver open the swing bridge to avoid being caught for the hit and run, or did the wind move it in a tragic coincidence?

Two days after the wrecks, the *Horry Herald* reported that whoever was driving the one-eyed Ford "was responsible for the wreck. In the opinion of some this man had gone on to the bridge and intended to block pursuit until his escape could be made good. He might not have meant to open the draw entirely, but only enough to stop the coming on of the other car while he made haste, perhaps, to get out of the country."

Perry Quattlebaum explained the bridge's safety at an inquest on September 11. It was his job "to open the bridge whenever a boat blew for it." When that happened, he retrieved the bridge key, which was kept "lying by the side of the bridge, right up about the center, up from the socket." Once the key was inserted, he would "walk around" to open it.

A crank operated the swing bridge manually, and the "key" Quattlebaum referred to was likely a long wrench or metal pole used as a crank handle. Another ice plant employee called it a "turn pole." When the operator walked in a circle pushing the pole, it cranked gears on a pivot mechanism set atop a concrete piling located under the bridge in the middle of the river, and the bridge opened.

Quattlebaum estimated the bridge was "sixty or seventy-five feet" long, and when he got it swung around far enough for watercraft to sail through he waited for the boat to pass. Then he cranked/walked the other direction until the bridge was closed again, and he "tied a couple of knots with a trace chain; it was tied on the end next to Conway."

If the key, or turn pole, was not used, Quattlebaum said, one man couldn't move the bridge by himself, but two probably could. He didn't think wind could move it far enough for a car to fall through, especially if the safety chain was in place.

"I don't think the wind would move it sixteen feet," he said. "It would have to move it sixteen feet for a car to go off it. It might move it a little bit one way or the other."

A few years earlier, Quattlebaum recalled, crew members from a boat named the *Dixie* opened the bridge at 11:00 p.m., and they didn't close it back up. The bridge remained open until 7:00 a.m. the next morning. In the period Quattlebaum had been the bridge tender, the only other time it was open when it wasn't supposed to be was a few years earlier, in September. A storm blew through, and "it was swung the length of the chain and a car couldn't go across it."

Quattlebaum was in charge of opening the bridge at night, and during "the day time it was turned by some of the laborers at the [ice] plant." Winston Russ, Quattlebaum said, had opened the bridge "a few times," with the most recent occasion he was aware of taking place "five or six weeks" earlier.

Dozens of people testified at the coroner's inquest held on September 11 at the county courthouse, which had a standing-room-only audience. Some said they previously saw the bridge moved by strong winds. Others said the bridge could only be manually moved without the turn pole if two or three men pulled on it. Another testified that more than five years earlier, a chain was put on the bridge to remedy the wind problem.

Quattlebaum said that in the ninety days preceding the tragedy, "the bridge had been repaired and prior to that time a heavy car would shake it." Z.L. Green said he had worked on the bridge on August 28 and for the previous week and a half and that it was in "very good" condition. When Green knocked off for the day at 6:00 p.m., the safety chain was "tied with a couple of knots. There was a big link and the chain was run through that big link."

Most everyone agreed it was unlikely that the bridge moved as far as it did that night without human intervention. J.H. Perry, who often crossed the bridge, said it was common for it to be out of place by "18 or 20 inches" but never more than that because the safety chain prevented it.

However, the chain had been dangling free, Perry Quattlebaum had noticed, right after the Connors' car fell into the river.

The One-Eyed Ford

Perry Quattlebaum said in his inquest testimony on September 11: "I think I saw a one-light car a few minutes before the alarm of the accident…After hearing the alarm I ran over there and found the draw span 15 or 20 feet from the approach. My chain was still hanging on the approach…Winston Russ had opened the bridge a few times while in our employ."

After the wreck, many people looked suspiciously at Winston Russ and his friends. Several testified they saw Russ pull up to the New York Café in downtown Conway at about 11:45 p.m. in a one-eyed Ford touring car owned by Julius Love. Love was a traveling salesman who lived in Sumter and worked for "a dry goods house" owned by M. Citron in Columbia. Russ, Love and another local young man named Frank Levinson stayed a short time at the café and then took the Ford to "Cushman's garage" before they returned to the café in a truck. A Conway police officer thought they also had a young woman with them.

J.A. Holt, the Conway officer, testified twice at the two coroner's inquests conducted on August 29 and September 11. The *Horry Herald* reported what he said on August 29:

> Last night about the time the storm came I was at the café corner and a car came to the café. Winston Russ, a travelling man, Mr. Levenson [sic] and a girl, maybe two. They stopped there and pretty soon they carried the car to Mr. Cushman's garage and did not tarry at café but a little while. Mr. Levenson and this other man and Russ took this little

one seated truck of Cushman's. They came to café and got a lunch and came back up the street…

About 12 o'clock and about 10 minutes after they came to [the] café [the] alarm was made at [the] Power plant and we got the fire engine out. We met Paul Quattlebaum who told him that some folks were drowned over at [the] steel bridge. No one [from Winston Russ's car] came to the alarm. John Chestnut and I went to get Russ and have him to explain what he knew about it. Bridge was closed when we got there.

Russ wanted to get [a] key from Levinson at [the] Hotel to open [the] garage to see [the] car. Russ and I went to room and he called for key. Levenson [sic] and the other man seemed to be very much excited when Levinson opened the door. He enquired what the trouble was, Russ told Levenson [sic] the car was wanted for purpose of investigation. The travelling man said they had not opened the bridge, and reminded Russ that he asked him whether the bridge would turn and Russ [said] yes, but we did not turn it. We got the keys and examined the lights and there was only one. On the right hand wheel there was a place that looked like it had been rubbed.

Officer Holt took the Ford's key and told the men to not move it. On September 11, Officer Holt elaborated on his earlier testimony.

I told [Russ] we wanted him to come down the street and go over to the bridge, that they were in trouble there and somebody said he was driving a car that wrecked a car and I asked him to come and tell what he knew about it. I asked him where that car was that he drove across the bridge and he said it was down in Cushman's garage. I said, "We want to examine it," he said "All right." I said "They claim the car that wrecked the other car was a car with only one light on it." He said, "The car I had been driving had two lights." I said, "We want to test it out."

We came to Kingston Hotel, [where] he said he had left the key with Frank Levinson or Julius Love. Russ and myself went to a room and we heard them [Levinson and Love] talking…Russ knocked at the door and they seemed very much excited and said, "What is the matter; what is the trouble?" I said, "There is a whole bunch of people drowned in the river and we want to get the key and examine that car you had been driving tonight; somebody ran into them over there and we want to examine the car you had been driving." Julius Love said to Russ, "Russ, I asked you if that bridge was turnable and you said yes, but we didn't turn it, did we?" And Russ said, "No."

They delivered the key and we went to the car to test it out. On the spokes of the right-hand front wheel there was a space of five or six spokes that had no mud on it, the whole wheel was muddy except that space that seemed to be rubbed around, the mud was all off it; it was rubbed perfectly clean, as clean as you could take anything and wipe it off. The spokes were not broke but the mud was wiped off near the hub…

Next morning I stopped the car and forbid him to move it until further orders, that it might be wanted at an investigation before the coroner's jury. Winston Russ said, "[Julius Love] has got to leave town." I said, "He can't leave in this car." I turned the key over to Mr. Cooper, the coroner, and I have not seen the car since.

THE LOVE CAR

Leona Jones (1903–1989) testified on September 11 that she was in the back seat of Julius E. Love's Ford with Joe Holliday and Frank Levinson. In the front seat were Julius Love, Max Banner and the driver, Winston Russ. She said they drove to Myrtle Beach from Conway after dark, got there around 9:00 p.m. and stayed about an hour and a half before heading back to Conway. Julius Love started off driving home, but in Socastee, while the car was slowly rolling, Love and Russ switched places. Russ took the driver's seat. She didn't know why Russ took over driving, and she said she didn't see anyone drinking alcohol that night.

The Love car arrived back in Conway at 11:40 p.m., Jones said, and her house was their first stop, where she got out and the five men drove away.

Joe Holliday remembered they left the beach around 10:30 p.m., and while he said they passed several cars along the way home, he stated, "We struck no other car." He recalled passing Marvin Connor in the Anderson mill area and named another car owner—Harry Bray—he recognized at the swing bridge but said he did not remember passing the Culliphers, whom he knew by sight.

Joseph William Holliday II (1901–1944) was the grandson of the original patriarch of a family that is still firmly established in Galivants Ferry. In the 1920s, his family had an extremely prosperous farm business; today, Holliday descendants still own much land in western Horry County, and many of their buildings are on the National Register of Historic Places. Anyone who has traveled west out of Horry County on U.S. 501 has seen their columned mansion, enormous three-story red-and-green barn and vintage mercantile on the east side of the Little Pee Dee River.

Joe Holliday was twenty-two years old in 1923. He later married Leona Jones, and they had a child.

Frank Levinson was in "the mercantile business," and Leona Jones was one of his store's three clerks. Julius Love, Levinson said at the inquiry, lived in Sumter and worked in a Columbia dry goods store. Love had arrived in Conway the morning of August 28. Levinson testified:

> *We left the beach and got to Anderson's mill and passed Mr. Conner [sic] in a car, and about a quarter mile up the road we passed another car, and I didn't see who was in that car. We came to town and got here right after the train came in, sometime between 11:30 and a quarter to 12, and we took Miss Jones home, and took Max Banner and Joe Holliday home.*
>
> *As we left his house it commenced to raining, and I said to Mr. Love, "Let's go to the café and get a night lunch before it closes." We got there about ten minutes to 12 and were eating lunch when Love said, "I've got to go to Little River in the morning," and Winston Russ said, "You can put your car in Cushman's place, and I will leave the key with you, and in case you want to leave early you can get your car."*
>
> *I took the key and went to the room after we put the car up. We were in the room and we heard the whistle blow, and I said, "I believe it is a fire." And I went to the window and didn't see any fire or smoke, and went back to my room and went to sleep…*
>
> *Later in the night the policeman came to my door, and we asked who it was, and he told us. I had the key to the car, and also to Cushman's garage, and he said, "We want the key to examine the Ford you all came in to town." I didn't ask him why he wanted the key, but gave him the key, and went back to bed. And that is all I know about it.*

When Max Banner testified about the evening's events, he said the young adults had gone to the Pavilion in Myrtle Beach, which was a popular oceanfront dancing and socializing spot. On the way home, they passed many cars, including Marvin Connor's Dort. However, he didn't know Sutton or Willie Cullipher and didn't know if they passed the Culliphers' Dort.

Winston Russ, who lived in Conway, gave the same timetable as his friends and said, "Down about eight miles from Conway we passed Mr. Connor in an old Dort car close to Mr. Anderson's saw mill, and came on about half or a quarter of a mile and we passed Mr. Cullipher. We left them behind and came on to the first bridge."

Russ said he was driving "about 30 or 35 miles an hour," while passing the Culliphers, and his questioner commented, "That is some going, isn't it?" Russ replied, "No." Also, despite Perry Quattlebaum testifying that Winston Russ had opened the bridge before, including just a few weeks prior to the tragedy, Russ denied it in the inquiry. He was asked if he had ever turned the bridge, and Russ's answer was, "Never in my life."

Russ also gave new information about witnesses who saw Julius Love's Ford cross the swing bridge:

> *On the other side of the veneering plant we passed a Hupmobile touring car. I heard later that Mr. Roscoe Gore was driving the car. He stopped and dimmed his light for us to go over the bridge. We crossed the drawbridge and passed Mr. Harry Bray and his wife going to the beach. I hollered to Mr. Bray, "Hey" and continued on into town, and put Miss Jones out, and then put Mr. Banner out and then Mr. Holliday, and drove straight back to the café and got a lunch and went to Mr. Cushman's place and hung around there for a few minutes, and put this car in the shed and hacked the roadster out.*
>
> *Mr. Elliott came along and asked me was I going home, and he got in my car and I went home straight, and about one o'clock they called me and pulled me out of bed.*

Mentioning that he saw Mr. and Mrs. Harry Bray seemed to exonerate the people in Julius Love's one-eyed Ford. Although the Brays were not called to testify at either inquest, the *Horry Herald* ran an article on September 20 headlined "Winston Russ Is Now Clear." It reads:

> *As Mr. and Mrs. Bray arrived at the steel bridge where the tragedy a little later occurred, and drew aside for a wagon to get off the bridge and were about to enter on the bridge, Mr. Bray saw another car entering the bridge at the other end of the draw, and the Bray car put on brakes and stopped close to the ditch while this oncoming car passed by.*
>
> *Some person in this passing car said, "Ha!"*
> *Mrs. Bray remarked to Mr. Bray: "That is someone who is drunk."*
> *Mr. Bray replied: "That sounds like Winston Russ."*
> *The names of Mr. and Mrs. Bray were handed in to the coroner as material witnesses to throw light on the bridge mystery. It was understood*

that they would be used as witnesses at the inquest, according to the statement of a citizen. It was expected that Mr. Harry Bray would be called to testify to show that it was not the driver of the one-eyed car who turned the bridge or wrecked the Cullipher car. Harry Bray would have testified that the voice he heard was that of Winston Russ.

[They] went over the bridge, and by the place where the Cullipher car was wrecked, a short time before the wreck took place, and the accident at the open draw a little later, and they will testify that they passed two cars just beyond the red hill from Conway. These two cars are supposed to have been the Cullipher and Conner [sic] cars.

They will testify that the car they met at the bridge had two lights in front.

…Suspicion has rested upon the occupants of the J.E. Love car driven into Conway on the fatal night by Winston Russ, a member of the party, the other members being J.E. Love, Frank Levinson, Maxey Banner, Miss Leona Jones and Joe Holliday. This new testimony unearthed and printed for the first time in this article will undoubtedly in the minds of all reasonable people clear up and put an end to all such suspicions.

The article concludes with the thought that the Little River Road branched off the road upon which the Culliphers and Connors were driving, between where the wreck occurred and the bridge. The one-eyed Ford, the article says, could have turned off on that road and never reached the bridge.

No Responsibility

The jury at the coroner's inquest released a verdict that said while it thought the Cullipher vehicle was wrecked by another car and that the swing bridge was opened by a human being that night, it did not have enough evidence to assign blame to anyone. The *Horry Herald* reported on September 27:

The jury placed no responsibility on any known person or persons for the opening of the draw. Their verdict was based on the testimony which has been published in this paper. It eliminates the theory that the bridge span was opened by the wind. It states that the span was opened by persons unknown to the jury and does not go any further for the reason that the testimony is not sufficient to fasten responsibility on any known person or persons.

On the other hand as to the wreck of the Cullipher car, on which the jury did not pass, it is abundantly established that the wrecking was done by human agency and not by accident as a result of careless steering. The man who wrecked the car and went on his way without stopping is as bad as the unknown person who turned the bridge.

Laid to Rest

The Culliphers' pastor was Reverend J.H. Causey of Loris. He was notified as soon as possible about the tragedy, but it wasn't in time for him to attend their funerals. Following the coroner's inquest held at the Kingston Furniture Co. on August 29, their bodies were taken to Nichols for burial.

Julius Sutton Cullipher and his wife, Cornelia Anna Cullipher, died with their three children on August 28, 1923, when the car they were in plunged into the Waccamaw River. *Author's collection.*

The entire family of Sutton and Cornelia Cullipher drowned just after midnight on August 28, 1923. *Author's collection.*

All five of the Culliphers are resting in Jones Nichols Cemetery, a quiet country spot just over the Horry County line in Marion County. The Culliper parents' gravestones each have a hand with one index finger pointing up. Sutton Culliper's marker says, "Father," with his name, dates of birth and death (November 28, 1892–August 28, 1923) and this epitaph: "'Twas hard to give thee up, But thy will of God be done."

Julius Sutton Culliper was survived by his parents, Mr. and Mrs. L.D. Culliper of Aynor; three brothers, Willie Culliper, A.T. Culliper and Arthur Culliper; and two sisters, Mrs. Mary Richardson of Brittons Neck and Mrs. Senie Huggins of Galivants Ferry.

Cornelia's stone is joined to his, and it says, "Mother," but her first name is misspelled—Conealia instead of Cornelia. It notes she was the "Wife of J.S. Culliper," and her birth and death dates (April 26, 1886–Aug. 28, 1923) are followed by "Asleep in Jesus." She was the daughter of Mr. and Mrs. Gilbert Price of Nichols.

The children's three separate markers, about one-sixth the size of their parents', each have a left-facing flying dove at the top followed by the word "BABY" in capital letters. Hettie was the eldest. She would have been eight years old in four more months. "Our loved one," her marker says. The middle child was also a daughter. Ella had just turned five, and her stone says she was "Gone to a better land." Two-year-old Julius G.'s epitaph is "Gone to sleep angel."

The drawbridge was used for fifteen more years before the current Main Street Bridge, which has two lanes and doesn't swing open, replaced it in 1938.

Top: Three tiny markers are in a line beside their parents at Jones Nichols Cemetery, where the Cullipher family was buried. *Author's collection*.

Right: Marvin Connor died seven years after the car he was driving plunged into the Waccamaw River, killing all six of his passengers. *Author's collection*.

Chapter 2

SUNSET LODGE AND OTHER BORDELLOS

The official Tom Yawkey website mentions the wealthy philanthropist's intelligence and caring nature, and you'd have a hard time finding anyone in Georgetown who would say otherwise about the man who owned the Boston Red Sox, established a wildlife refuge, financially supported the Tara Hall Home for Boys and hugely financed Georgetown Memorial Hospital in 1950. But what the site doesn't mention is that he introduced to Georgetown one of the East Coast's most infamous bordellos: the Sunset Lodge.

SOCIAL REMEDY

At age sixteen in 1919, Tom Yawkey (1903–1976) inherited about $21 million from his uncle/adoptive father, William Hoover Yawkey, Ben Bradlee Jr. explained in *The Kid: The Immortal Life of Ted Williams*. Part of the inheritance was a thirty-one-square-mile estate near Georgetown that includes parts of North, South and Cat Islands. In 1933, at age thirty, Yawkey was able to control all of his inheritance. Four days later, he bought the Boston Red Sox.

Yawkey often traveled by train to Florence, South Carolina, before continuing seventy miles to the waterfront retreat where he liked to fish, hunt and enjoy solitude. He also enjoyed patronizing prostitutes, and Florence had a thriving red-light district. That's where he made a proposal to Hazel Weisse, who worked at a "sporting house."

Tom Yawkey married Elise Sparrow in 1938. They later divorced, and he remarried. *Photograph by William C. Greene. Library of Congress, Prints & Photographs Division, NYWT&S Collection.*

Being a "sporting lady," which was a euphemism of the day for a prostitute, hadn't always been Weisse's occupation. Born Hazel Bennett in 1900 in a small community at the northern end of the Hoosier National Forest, she was a schoolteacher in her native state of Indiana before deciding there was an easier way to be more prosperous.

Susan Atkinson* of Georgetown County was a frequent visitor at the Sunset Lodge, due to a business relationship, and says Weisse explained her background.

> [Weisse's] *parents both were real, real sick. She tried to teach school and take care of them. She was out one day hanging clothes on the line, this is what she told us. She said she was out there one day, and it was freezing raining, and* [by] *the time she'd hang one up it would freeze. The whole line was hanging there frozen. She said, "This is not for me. I am not going to live like this. I've got an education, and I'm going to get out of it."*
>
> *Very shortly after that her mother and dad died, one right behind the other. She went to this particular house* [of ill repute] *up north, and that's where she met Mr. Yawkey for the first time. She was working as a prostitute. She had just got going. He knew she was educated; she was the only educated woman in that house. He brought her to Florence to get her settled, and he had this place ready in Georgetown before he brought her here.*

Tom Yawkey was married (twice), but as he and Weisse grew closer, he may have been looking for a way to have his lady-friend nearer to his Georgetown

The Sunset Lodge was just south of Georgetown right off Highway 17. *Matt Silfer, Silfer Studios.*

property. When International Paper started building a huge plant at the south end of town, civic leaders were concerned that rough northern construction workers would improperly approach their southern belles. A cathouse, they decided, was the perfect solution to tame their romantic feelings.

Yawkey said he'd handle that civic duty, and he told Hazel Weisse he'd stake her in business if she'd move to Georgetown. Some people say he loaned her the money and she paid it back promptly while others say he was the sole financier and gave the property to Weisse. Whichever was the case, the Sunset Lodge made Hazel Weisse a wealthy woman.

Atkinson had a family friend whose mother was a bootlegger, and "she got caught so many times running illegal whiskey to them they were going to run her out of town." This bootlegger had a four-bedroom house south of town on a fifteen-acre plot beside Highway 17.

Tom Yawkey bought the bootlegger's property, and the house was quickly readied for business before it opened in 1936.

Shipshape Business

While the business wasn't legal, Atkinson said Weisse ran a tight ship:

> *She gathered her girls up before getting to Georgetown. The first time I ever saw her, I had never seen anybody with as pretty copper-colored hair as she had. It just looked like it had gold in it. It was natural. She was a big woman, very attractive. Not pretty so much, but so attractive. She became the madam out there, and she got her first set of girls out there. It didn't take any time that the construction workers* [at International Paper] *knew exactly where to go. Miss Hazel ran a very tight house. She was just like a sergeant in the army. She conducted everything, and everybody listened. Miss Hazel walked the line on 'em. They didn't get anything on her. She had the town snowed: the officials, the lawyers, the doctors. She had everybody of any knowledgeable position, she had them under her wing, and they listened to Miss Hazel. She paid off well.*

Atkinson's description of Weisse's physical appearance is kind; others have said she was plain, homely or even ugly. She was also called tall and statuesque. But no one disputes Hazel Weisse was so kempt, so charming and so generous that she was attractive to people.

Rebecca T. Godwin wrote an extremely entertaining novel based on the Sunset Lodge titled *Keeper of the House*, and it was published in 1995 under St. Martin's Griffin label. Susan Atkinson says while a few parts of *Keeper of the House* are fiction, most of the descriptions are accurate.

The Sunset Lodge really did have a housekeeper named Minyon, or Minnie, as described in the novel. There was a cook named Sarah, and Ophelia cooked and did other chores. Those three Sunset employees were African American, along with a bartender/bouncer/handyman named Frank. Atkinson said:

> *Minnie came from right out here at Arcadia. When* [Weisse and Tom Yawkey] *went out there to get her, Mr. Yawkey had told her about this young black girl. Hard-working girl. She needed to get out, because she was in an abusive family. Her grandmother adored her, but she could only do so much. Minnie was not educated, but she was smart. Hazel decided that they did not want to call her Minnie, because that was common. She said, "Minyon is your name." Like filet mignon.*
>
> *Ophelia carried* [all the bed sheets] *home and cleaned them, and they smelled good. She hung them on the line—that had to be some kinda damn long line, to hold all them sheets. They kept count of the sheets being cleaned, and that's how they knew how many people had been there and how much taxes was owed. The IRS checked the sheets. That was the neat way to do it, because Miss Hazel was clean. Everybody got a clean sheet.*

Sarah, Ophelia and Frank didn't live at Sunset Lodge, but Minnie did. The sporting ladies also boarded at the world-famous "sporting house" of course, and Atkinson said most of them were in their profession because they grew up uneducated and poor. This line of work was the best available option in their judgments. Susan Atkinson says the greatest number of girls she knew to be working at the Sunset at one time was fifteen and the least was eight. Since the main house had only a few bedrooms, business was mostly conducted in small freestanding cabins behind the house.

The two-story wood house's exterior was rather normal in appearance—striped awnings over the windows and a low brick fence around a tidy yard. Men from humble backgrounds were impressed by what they viewed as the house's interior opulence while others said the interior was not spectacular. A huge and ornate mirror hung on the wall of the main parlor, and there was an enormous sofa that encouraged canoodling. A small bar with a multicolor backlight and a jukebox created a carefree atmosphere.

Knowing the Customers

When Tom Yawkey visited the Sunset Lodge, he was the only person allowed to bring his dog inside the house, Atkinson said. It waited at the foot of the stairs while Yawkey visited Miss Hazel, his paramour, in her room.

"Mr. Yawkey never used any other girl," Atkinson said. "Strictly Hazel. When he drove up to that yard, she just lit up like crazy. She was his woman."

Some men who visited were heavily scrutinized. They might have been paying eight dollars per hour for sex with beautiful women, but they had to act civilized and be clean. Atkinson said:

> *They watched the men like hawks. I don't know that many were turned away, because the ones that went had the money to pay, and money was the thing. She was there to make money. But* [Weisse] *was so clean, and them men had to be clean when they went in there. She made sure that they did. I've seen them have to go back out and have a cold water shower; if she didn't like the looks of them she made them clean up.*
>
> *Do you see this pan here?* [Atkinson held up a round metal-enameled pan of the sort someone would use for shelling beans.] *That's a "peter pan." They washed in it. There were stacks of 'em like this at the door when you went in. Each man took a pan off, and there was a big old thing with solution that looked like the bottled water you get now. It was a big tank you could see through, and it had a solution in it. Everyone took a pan, and they went in that room and they washed. She made damn sure they washed their penis off before she let them in a room.*

Local lawmen were frequent visitors, Atkinson said, along with doctors, lawyers, judges, politicians, accountants, shopkeepers and tradesmen. One week every spring, the Sunset Lodge was closed to the public and "available only to Members of the General Assembly and the judiciary," wrote Robert A. Pierce in 1989 in the *State* newspaper. Elizabeth Robertson Huntsinger wrote for *Tidelands* magazine in 2002 that "one week each spring was set aside for members of the South Carolina General Assembly and the judiciary. During this week the lodge was closed to the public with a chain drawn across the driveway." Pierce said another tradition was "Hazel's birthday party in October when Georgetown's social register—but men only—attended, by invitation only." Everything was on the house that night.

Part of Weisse's business acumen included knowing her clientele and showing them appreciation for allowing her to stay in business. Certain influential and helpful customers—especially lawmen—received lavish holiday gifts, such as a leather desk set or a case of whiskey or a lot of cash. Each year, she bought a new Buick and was given first pick at the dealership. Local businesses happily sold her supplies. She contributed generously to just about every local charity that asked, from the United Way to the Red Cross.

OUT AND ABOUT

Alzata Lee of Murrells Inlet remembers the Sunset Lodge girls coming into Lee's Inlet Kitchen to eat, and that they were beautiful and well dressed. But Hazel Weisse was never with them, she said.

Sometimes Tom Yawkey brought Boston Red Sox athletes to his Georgetown home on the way to spring training, and Miss Hazel shut down Sunset Lodge and sent the girls over to entertain the players. Other wealthy Yawkey friends cruised by in their yachts to pick girls up and take them off for hijinks on the high seas.

While satisfied investors, lawmen and locals were important for keeping the Sunset Lodge in business, it was soldiers who put it on the map. Thousands of soldiers who trained in the area during World War II found their ways to the Sunset Lodge. It became so well known, local soldiers who were sent to Europe or the Pacific could say they were from Georgetown, South Carolina, and often the response was, "Sunset Lodge!"

The business's notoriety was due to Hazel Weisse's giving customers what they wanted, and they wanted gorgeous girls. Hundreds of girls, who used aliases, worked there over the decades, and usually they were rotated out every three months. Susan Atkinson recalls hardworking girls whose families thought their daughters and sisters were working in a factory or at a summer vacation resort.

These girls were from different parts of the world. A great many of them for some reason were from West Virginia, up in the coal mine area. They were all beautiful people. Beautiful. Skin like peaches and cream. Some of them couldn't write their name. They just didn't have an education, but they were attractive. They didn't know anything else to do with their bodies. They couldn't go work in a department store. They couldn't go to a restaurant and work. All they could do was whatever they knew to do on their backs.

Miss Hazel took 'em in, and she was good to them. She saw that they had the very best of food that could be bought. They had the very best of clothes [that] could be bought. I don't know why, but they loved strapless shoes, and they would go and they would all wear strapless shoes.

Most of the women sent the majority of their earnings to their families back home, but they had enough left over to spread their cash around town. They always paid in cash.

A local department store kept a special selection of negligees in stock for them, and a specific employee was designated to always wait on the ladies. "It wasn't whorish red and black fur," June Williams*, who worked at the department store, said. "It was elegant. Blues and cream, iridescents, their nightclothes were something else…when these girls came in they were gorgeous. They were refined."

If the women didn't arrive with social skills, Weisse tutored them.

"She took them like they were her schoolchildren and she was a college mom," Atkinson said. "She made sure they was schooled, she made sure they knew how to use their dinnerware, pick up the right knife and fork."

BEHIND THE SCENES

While Weisse could be compassionate, she was a shrewd businesswoman. She didn't allow her employees to get emotionally close enough to hug or touch her, and she took care that all of them maintained low profiles while out in the community.

Each lady of the evening normally serviced eight to ten men per night, and there was a rush for the staff to get the sheets changed between men. In later years, when the amount of sheets became too numerous for Ophelia to wash, a laundry service handled them.

The Internal Revenue Service, Atkinson said, continued to use a sheet count to determine how much tax Weisse owed. How an illegal business was legally taxed remains a mystery, but Atkinson says Weisse regularly handed over thousands in cash to the various men who allowed her to operate.

To promote health and to help prevent pregnancy, the women used an acidic potash douche after turning each trick. But still, some of the ladies were impregnated. Atkinson recalls one having an abortion after a physician gave her a drug called Ergoapiol.

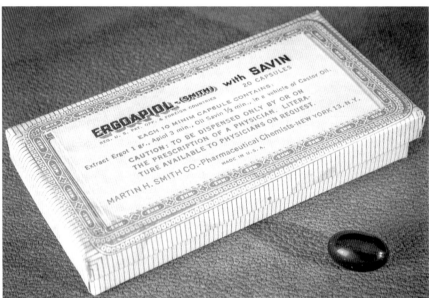

Unwanted pregnancies at the Sunset Lodge were sometimes eliminated when a physician prescribed Ergoapiol. *Photographs by Matt Silfer, Silfer Studios.*

One baby was born at Sunset Lodge. Atkinson recalls:

> *She was a very poor girl, and she did not have anywhere to go. Miss Hazel said she could not keep this girl there, that she could not have a baby in the*

house. At first the baby stayed out back with Minnie. They helped raise that baby. But Miss Hazel had to put her foot down. She said, "We cannot keep this child here. This is a house that we have to hold up. It's called ladies of the night. We can't have a baby."

But they kept that baby. But then the baby was not quite a year old, and she said, "Well I'll have to do something." The girl had no place to go. She had no family or money. If she did have family, they didn't claim her and they probably didn't want a baby anyway. So Miss Hazel contacted somebody up north. She bought that girl—this is the kind of woman she was—she bought that girl a ticket, she got her an apartment up north in this town. She got somebody to take care of her baby and she sent her to a school to learn to read and write. She finally ended up working in an insurance office. That's the kind of woman Miss Hazel was. She had a heart of gold, but honey you didn't stomp on it.

Interesting Characters

Keeping her heart's core protected was probably wise considering the Sunset Lodge's diverse ladies and their place in Georgetown society hierarchy. They were all Caucasian except for one mixed-race woman, and she didn't stay long because the other ladies shunned her. Another had a snake tattoo winding around her torso that she could make slither with certain movements.

Then there was Grace.

"Grace was a beautiful girl," Atkinson said. "She didn't smile a lot, but she was very, very, very religious…When the men would come get in the bed with her and they would go ahead and have their fun, she'd look up, and she'd say 'Thank you Jesus! Thank you God! Thank you for giving this poor soul relief. I know his soul's going to go to heaven. He doesn't get it at home, and I'm here for him, and thank you Lord.'"

During her business dealings with Sunset Lodge, Atkinson became close with a sporting lady named Becky. Eventually, she felt comfortable enough to ask Becky something she wondered about for years.

When we went in, stacked by every one of those beds was a mat. It was a little longer [than a kitchen table], and it was green. It was like a little mattress. They would put the beds so high up off the floor, and the mats were stacked up on top of each other. There would be like five or six under each bed. For ages and ages I didn't know what in the world that was, so I asked Becky. She said some of the men come in and have back problems. They don't do it on the bed; they want it on the floor. And they pulled that mattress out, put it down beside the bed, and that's where the intercourse took place.

QUIET PROTECTION

Most of the prominent local men who patronized Sunset Lodge were also churchgoers. So how was it that the Sunset managed to be a fringe factor in the Georgetown community for so many years?

Tom Yawkey wanted the Sunset Lodge, and he spread cash thickly. People credit his money for building Georgetown Memorial Hospital, and there are many charities and individual hard-luck cases that received his funding.

Susan Atkinson had a friend whose child was born with a severe physical anomaly. Yawkey heard of their situation and took action.

"He made sure that they had hired help to go to that house and help change her bandages," Atkinson said. "He made sure they had proper help."

While the wives of Georgetown knew the cathouse existed, it was understood that when it came to the Sunset Lodge, complaining publicly was not condoned in light of how much Yawkey and Weisse contributed financially to the community—at least, that was the official reason. There's no denying many local men thoroughly enjoyed patronizing the Sunset. It was known as a clean and upper-class bordello with white female prostitutes and white male customers. Nurses visited the Lodge twice a month to check the ladies for gonorrhea and syphilis, and if they were disease free, they got a health certificate that was displayed under glass on their bedside tables.

"Everybody knew it existed," Atkinson said, "but it was 'hands off.' Even the women couldn't say much about it. They might grumble to one another." It wasn't unusual for residents to make protecting Miss Hazel and her customers a team effort.

A lot of Georgetown men went during the week, because it was better for them. One of them was a very, very prosperous businessman in Georgetown…He was a frequent out there, and he and Miss Hazel were good friends…He told his wife, "I have a meeting at the Francis Marion Hotel in Charleston, and I'm going to have to leave. I won't be back until late." Well, she believed him, so he left. One of her friends came by and said, "I think I'm going to ride to Mount Pleasant and Charleston, if you want to ride with me." The wife said, "Well, I better not, because I need to do some things." When the friend got back she called the wife and said, "Well what was your car doing sitting out there at the Sunset?"

The wife insisted that couldn't be their car at the Sunset Lodge, but the more she thought about it, the more she felt compelled to ride out there and see for herself. Somehow word spread quickly that this woman was headed to the Sunset to find her husband.

"This man's wife is on the way out there, and she's going to raise hell when she gets there," Atkinson said. "So quick-thinking Miss Hazel, she called an ambulance. The ambulance [which doubled as a hearse] went out there, and he laid down in there, and it carried him home. He got there, and his wife wasn't there—she was out looking for him at the Sunset."

When the wife returned home, the husband explained he had a flat tire on the way to Charleston and had to leave their car at the Sunset.

A similar tale was recounted by Lillian Mills* of Myrtle Beach. She remembers a Myrtle Beach motel owner who traveled each year to a plant nursery in Florida. Hitched to his vehicle was a trailer that he'd load up with plants and bring back to spruce up the motel grounds.

One year, Mills said, he arrived home and discovered he didn't have his trailer with him.

"They searched high and low for that trailer," Mills said. "He thought somebody had stolen it. And guess what—they found it parked at the Sunset Lodge. He left it at the Sunset Lodge on his way home. He thought someone had stolen it, but he couldn't remember where he left it. He must have had a jolly good time."

Another story involves a Georgetown storeowner who provided supplies to the Sunset. He sent his young teenage son out there with a delivery, and when he got there, the girls, who were dressed in normal daytime clothing, asked him if he'd like to play cards. He accepted and stayed quite a long while.

His mother started wondering where her son was. When her husband told her that he was sent to the Sunset Lodge with a delivery, Susan Atkinson says her reaction was to say, "I'll give him thirty minutes. If he's not back, you go and get him or I'm going."

Thirty minutes passed, and the son hadn't returned. In the meantime, word got around town that the mother planned to go fetch her son and would likely cause a scene.

"The police got word that [she] was going out to Sunset, so they went and parked their cars in front of her driveway, and she couldn't get out," Atkinson said. "They blocked her all the way across. That's just how much they protected it," Atkinson said. "Everybody protected Miss Hazel. Everybody."

The father drove out to the Sunset and told the son to hightail it home.

NO PUBLIC SUPPORT

Although Hazel Weisse had the protection of powerful men, that association usually didn't extend to fraternizing in public. One year, the girls were excited about an annual summer parade that Weisse supported financially, and they wanted to go see it. Weisse piled several into her shiny Buick, and they drove to town.

> Those girls got so excited, because they saw some of the men sitting up on the back of the fire truck in the parade. Other men were driving cars, and they were people who had been going to the Sunset for years. The girls would wave at them, and they wouldn't wave back. The fire chief was sitting there driving the truck, and the girls went, "Heeeeeeey!" But they wouldn't even wave back…One girl was so upset that a certain Mister wouldn't speak to her, she passed out on the sidewalk. Miss Hazel got her in that car, and she told Minnie, "You drive this car straight back to the house." She hated causing a scene.

However, there was at least one notable exception to the rule about fraternizing outside the Sunset's walls.

> There was one girl out there, and she was not a—she was not really young like the others. But the men liked her. There was this one man in Georgetown, his wife had cancer, and he would go out to the Sunset and ask for this girl. He was very good to his wife. She had everything. But he did go out to the Sunset, and every time he went he would ask for this particular woman. Well, she fell in love with him, and he fell in love with her. But he did not leave his wife. When she died, he went back, and he asked Miss Hazel, he said, "I'm in love with her and I want to take her out of here and I want her for my wife." She said, "I don't think that that will work for you." He said, "Well, I want you to see if you can't help me with it. I

*will take good care of her, and I promise she will never want for anything."
Well, after a while, Miss Hazel broke down and told him that she would
agree to that, so he took the lady and he married her. Everywhere they went
he drove her around, and when they went to the restaurants…he opened that
car door for her to get out. He treated her so beautifully…He adored her.*

Three Decades and Done

A few days before Christmas 1969, Sheriff Woodrow Carter closed down
the Sunset Lodge. Some say he was fulfilling a campaign promise; others
say the closure had to do with civil rights and integration. Either way, it
happened in a hurry, Atkinson said.

"They had one call, and Hazel told them to get their belongings together.
They had to get out. She had a big truck coming, and they went so fast and took
everything they had. They put everything in bureau drawers, and they took the
whole drawer and put them in the truck. That truck took them to Florence, I
think, and they went from there. That's how fast they had to leave."

And just like that, the thirty-three-year run of the Sunset Lodge was over.
Weisse sold the property in 1970, and for a while, she stayed there in an
apartment. Some of her girls came back to visit. After the Sunset closed, she
took care of the person who spent the prime of her life living and working at
the Sunset and being Miss Hazel's number-one assistant: Minyon.

"Minnie was getting old, too," Atkinson said. "Miss Hazel wanted her to
have a little house in Georgetown, so she bought her a neat little house. A
solid little small house…and Miss Hazel fixed it so the taxes and everything
on it was paid for as long as she lived. All Minnie had to do was buy her food,
and Miss Hazel left a small salary for that."

Weisse's son never lived at the Sunset. He attended a boarding school in
Charleston, and as far as Atkinson knows, he didn't learn what his mother did
for a living until he was an adult. Her obituary ran in the *Georgetown Times* on
July 23, 1974, with the headline "Mrs. Weisse Dies Monday After Illness."

*Mrs. Hazel Weisse, former Georgetown resident, died Monday in an
Indianapolis, Ind. hospital following a long illness. The funeral was
conducted there by the George Herman Funeral Home. Mrs. Weisse, who
would have been 74 on October 28 of this year, is survived by a son, two
grandchildren and several great-grandchildren.*

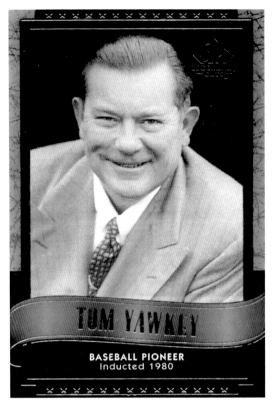

TOM YAWKEY

BASEBALL PIONEER
Inducted 1980

Tom Yawkey, who helped launch the Sunset Lodge in Georgetown, owned the Boston Red Sox and was posthumously inducted into the National Baseball Hall of Fame in 1980. *Author's collection.*

Tom Yawkey passed away in 1976 in Boston and the Sunset Lodge burned down in 1993. Yawkey left his waterfront Georgetown property, the Tom Yawkey Wildlife Center Heritage Preserve, for future generations of wildlife lovers. Guided tours of its twenty-four thousand acres of marshland, beach and maritime forest are reserved well in advance. In 2013, the Thomas A. Yawkey Foundation had assets of more than $66 million, and it gave charity grants totaling $2,696,497.

SEX SELLS

While the Sunset Lodge was the most infamous area bordello, the sex trade has been going on a long time in Horry County (but we still don't pronounce the *h*—it's silent).

In colonial times, often a person's skin color revealed sexual activity, such as when white masters or overseers raped female slaves and resulted in pregnancies. Bordellos existed in Charleston, where sailors sought them out, and the port cities of Georgetown and Little River had rooms over some city taverns and at roadside ordinaries where sailors, fishermen and travelers found comfort and quite possibly carried away a venereal disease. In those days, prostitution was legal.

Immediately following the Civil War, white and black couples who had sex (or even just held hands) might be punished by the Ku Klux Klan. "The Klan punished Negroes who associated with low white women," David Chalmers wrote in *Hooded Americanism*. "White prostitutes in South Carolina accused of receiving Negroes were tarred and driven away. A Negro was killed and his daughter whipped because she 'had caused embarrassment' to a white family by bearing the child of one of its members. Another Negro girl was beaten for 'breaking the peace' between a wife and her husband."

A 1913 article in the *Horry Herald* with the headline "Notorious Place Has Been Closed" explained how a business called Bill's Place, on Ocean Drive in the present-day North Myrtle Beach area, was shut down by the sheriff's office after being under investigation by the FBI.

> *The place had a bad reputation. Off and on sheriff's officers had picked up some seventy women, going back to January, and twenty of these came from Bill's Place. Bill's Place was warned several times to discontinue. The place was watched by FBI officers as well as by state officers.*
>
> *Sometime ago the Sheriff found two girls both under sixteen years of age, who had run away from their homes in Ohio and were putting up at this place. Sheriff's officers took the girls in charge and they were returned to their homes.*
>
> *A warrant was issued for Bill's arrest but he was given his choice of going to jail or closing the place and leaving the county. At last accounts he had nailed up the place and could not be found anywhere in the county.*
>
> *Citizens have complained about this place for about the space of one year passed.*

In the 1920s, when the Ku Klux Klan was a dominant force in politics, its politicians ran on platforms firmly against prostitution, but that didn't stop bordellos from staying in business. Lillian Mills* remembers one in Myrtle Beach that she says was almost as notorious as the Sunset Lodge.

"You know where Pridgen Road is? It comes into Highway 15. Right at the end of that road was a little dinky house, but it had little cottages around it, and supposedly, it was a motel…It was called Bobbi Jean's. In our area, they say, 'Well, did you go to Bobbi Jean's or did you go to Sunset?' It was a common thing of the day."

In the early days of transportation, many service stations were built with rooms upstairs, where the station owner could live. After more modern gas stations began to replace them, the old ones were sometimes converted to cathouses. Mills remembers one such station a little north of Ramsey Acres in Myrtle Beach. Another was along the main drag in Murrells Inlet.

Alzata Lee, born in 1928, is a Murrells Inlet native who remembers her mother not letting her walk past a certain establishment when she was about eight years old. The building is still there today. It has been Lee's Inlet Kitchen since 1948.

But in 1936, it was a filling station typical of the day. The two-story cottage hugged the road in front of it, and it had two bedrooms upstairs for the proprietors. Lee and her friend Genevieve Chandler Peterkin were under strict orders from their mothers to not walk near it.

"What we'd do is we'd get in the ditch and walk to the side," she said, "because the women would be out there drunk, the men would be out there drunk."

The owner of the filling station was from Mullins, Lee said, and he brought his working girls from over that way. They weren't locals, she emphasized. In fact, locals got fed up with the public displays of hedonism, and they let the fellow from Mullins know he wasn't welcome. Eventually, the property was abandoned, and Eford Lee bought it for a bargain price in a public tax sale. He and his wife, Pearl, raised their children in those two bedrooms over the former filling station, which they turned into the restaurant Lee's Inlet Kitchen.

The original building has been enlarged several times, but those upstairs bedrooms are still there. Alzata Lee remembers curtains fluttering in their screen-less openings when she was an eight-year-old scrambling through ditches to avoid getting too close. She was the first waitress at Lee's Inlet Kitchen in 1948, and in 2015, she was still working there as a hostess while the third generation of Lees owned and operated it.

In the 1970s and '80s, the woman to know was Miss Jinx. She was a madam whose house of ill repute was on Flagg Street near the Rivoli Theater.

"Jinx was red-headed, short," Richard Williams* said. "She was beefy, but not in a bad way. Rubenesque would be the term."

Williams was the maître d' at one of Myrtle Beach's finest hotel restaurants where, in the early 1970s, they were fetching $14.50 for a jumbo shrimp cocktail and $25.00 for a steak and offered tableside service for dishes such as crêpes and flambés.

"People would get the bill, and they would gasp," he said.

One time, about a dozen British men visited, and they asked Williams if he could bring them "some company."

"I knew what he was talking about, and I said, 'It's better if you talk to the doorman about that.' And he gave me a $100 bill and he said, 'Would you talk to the doorman for me?'"

Williams did talk to the doorman, and soon the phone rang in the restaurant. It was Miss Jinx, and she told Williams that she and the girls would arrive within an hour at staggered intervals and seat themselves at different areas of the restaurant. Soon several gorgeous and impeccably dressed women were laughing and talking with the men, and the party lasted for several days with chateaubriand for lunchtime room service, fruit trays, dessert trays and a copious river of champagne.

"It was unbelievable, the bills," Williams said, adding he made hundreds of dollars in tips that week. "I was going in on days off to take care of things and handle stuff. One guy bought one of the girls a Mustang and wanted to marry her, and I think she left with him."

Chapter 3
SILLY TOURISTS

Myrtle Beach–area locals love the income tourists bring, but a percentage of the millions of annual visitors also bring bad behavior. Some are running away and come to Myrtle Beach to blend in

The millions of visitors who arrive each year to enjoy Grand Strand beaches sometimes act silly. *Photograph by Matt Silfer, Silfer Studios.*

with the crowds and relax. Some act rotten at home and are no different (or maybe worse) when on vacation. Some are respectable at home, but they figure they can get by with acting horrible in a community where no one knows them. Others act stupid because they're intoxicated. Still more are just silly.

BODY ON DISPLAY

And some are silly without even trying. In 1934, a young bank employee from Marion, Frank Salmon, drove his car filled with friends to Myrtle Beach for a weekend house party. He had a trailer hooked to his car that contained a "leather covered day bed which resembled a casket."

In May 1934, gangster and bank robber John Dillinger was two months away from being shot to death by FBI agents and was at the height of his notoriety. Dillinger sightings swirled throughout the United States.

Salmon parked his car and trailer in Conway for a short time while he picked up a friend, and the rumor quickly spread through the community that gangsters connected with Dillinger were in town, and they had a body in a casket with them—as if gangsters would haul around a body, in a coffin, in an open trailer.

Conway police officers contacted Myrtle Beach police officers and told them to be on the lookout for the vehicle. "Six or more officers in automobiles and on motorcycles with screaming sirens" went looking for the car, the *Field* reported. The officers got to the party house shortly after Salmon, saw there was a misunderstanding and "enjoyed a hearty laugh at the joke they had perpetrated upon themselves."

CREATIVE VACATION FINANCING

Sometimes people get money for their Myrtle Beach vacations in unusual ways. Out of booze? Rob a liquor store. Hungry? Walk out on your restaurant bill. Need to pay for a week's stay? Boost a car at home and sell it at the beach.

In 1951, J.B. Strickland and John A. Drew were caught selling hot cars from North Carolina in the Grand Strand area, the Conway *Field & Herald* reported. The "auto theft ring" was caught after the FBI issued an alert to law enforcement to look for a certain car stolen in Jacksonville, North Carolina. A short time later, South Carolina State Highway patrolman William B. Wetherington spotted the car near Conway, and "a wild chase" ensued that ended in the Ocean Drive section of North Myrtle Beach.

When caught, Strickland gave up without a fight, and then officers discovered a ".25 caliber automatic pistol" and a German luger, both fully loaded, in the car. Six stolen 1950 Fords and Chevrolets were recovered in "Myrtle Beach, Crescent Beach and Loris where Strickland had sold them directly to individual motorists."

It's common for thieves to break into cars parked at public beach parking areas along the coast. Sometimes, people foolishly leave their cars unlocked, and other times, the robbers commit quick smash-and-grabs. During May and October, when thousands of motorcycle enthusiasts visit the Grand Strand area, there are usually reports of motorcycles being picked up out of hotel parking lots, placed in vans or trailers and driven quickly out of town. Sometimes they're caught and sometimes not.

Another common type of theft perpetrated by Grand Strand visitors or drifters is the swindle. Usually business owners are targeted, and the thieves are bold.

In an article headlined "Georgetown Hotel Victim of New Type Swindle," the *Field & Herald* reported in March 1951 that Creel O. Robinson was known for calling hotels and pretending to be a jockey working for a wealthy horse owner. In those days before ATMs, part of his scheme was to secure a "cash advance" for himself upon arrival.

Georgetown police chief F.E. Nobles was paraphrased as saying, "Robinson jumped a board and room bill in Conway, where he represented himself as a 'commander in the army.' According to the Conway rooming house owner, Robinson said he was there to reopen the airfield."

In another gutsy type of swindle, a Myrtle Beach restaurateur's love of celebrities cost him an expensive meal.

We've all been to restaurants where the walls are plastered with photographs of celebrities who've eaten there. For about twenty years, there was such a place in Myrtle Beach. Some of the photographs were of just the celebs, but in many, the restaurant owner was also in them, with his arm around the stars.

A few years into the twenty-first century, a man visited that restaurant and saw all the photographs. This man had been told by friends that he resembled a certain movie and television star, and it was his habit to dress like that star and carry himself like a VIP. He liked it when people mistook him for the celebrity.

So the man didn't waste any time telling the star-struck restaurant owner that he was, in fact, that famous actor, and the restaurateur plied the man and his companions with free food and drinks. Then he asked for a photograph of himself with the "star." The man complied.

The entire ruse might have gone unnoticed, except that the restaurant owner used the photograph in a newspaper advertisement, and thousands of people recognized that the man in the image wasn't the celebrity he claimed to be.

NON-FLYING EXPERIENCE

Two teenagers and a twenty-year-old from New Jersey decided in June 1952 to go to the Myrtle Beach Airport and steal a Stinson four-passenger airplane. They "cranked the plane up without untying the ropes that tied it down," a newspaper article says, and "the right wing broke, causing the plane to whirl around sharply to the right."

The plane taxied out of the hangar, and then "the left wing of the plane struck a telephone pole, causing the plane to turn around and reenter the hangar where it crashed into a plane owned by John Underwood, Jr. Both planes were practically demolished...The three youths, unhurt, jumped out of the wrecked plane and ran to an automobile."

They were no better at driving a car than they were driving a plane. The kids ran the car into a ditch, and the trio was caught and arrested.

CROWD CONTROL

Put thousands of people on vacation in a small area, and it's inevitable that some will act up. Spring break crowds are a special entity with the ages of the visitors contributing to mayhem, but even family-type crowds can have problems.

In June 1962, the *Sun News* reported that a crowd of 400,000 was expected for the Sun Fun Festival during its five days of oceanfront events, and a similar number was estimated to be in the Grand Strand that year during the Fourth of July week. The hotels and campgrounds were so full that many people slept in their cars and on the beach. Restaurants had long lines of people waiting their turns to be fed. Grocery store checkout lines stretched for 350 feet.

A *Sun News* reporter interviewed Earl Husted, manager of the Myrtle Beach Pavilion, who said, "We had more people on the rides than any single day in the history of the park. They started early Monday evening and didn't let up until we closed down. It is the largest crowd ever on the beach."

With so many people in town, business owners and police officers marveled that most everyone was extremely well mannered, and it was theorized that this was because there were fewer drinkers than normal.

"Liquor store operators said their business was off," the article says. "This fact may reflect in the observations of other merchants who called the 'crowd different from in the past,' and the police who termed the vacationers 'exceptionally orderly.' The lack of activity in the liquor stores might also be reflected in the difficulty of renting houses for a week. 'We haven't had the big spender who bought from $18 to $25 worth of liquor at a time,' one dealer said."

Here Comes Da Fish

"The irresistible urge for fresh water fish had been costly," an article in the July 26, 1962 *Sun News* says. Three visitors from Florence let their appetites get them into trouble.

The men were on a weekend visit in Surfside Beach, and on Friday night, they stopped by a grocery store to buy shrimp.

When the clerk walked into a rear room to fetch the shrimp, the men followed her. They saw two fine-looking strings of fish in the walk-in refrigerator, and they asked if they were for sale. They weren't, the clerk said. They belonged to her boss.

Two of the men went up front to pay for the shrimp, but the third took the fish and left by way of a back door.

The clerk didn't mention her boss's name to the men; it was Magistrate Wallace Harrelson.

By Saturday, one man had been found, and he confessed. He was given instructions to bring the fish and his two friends to the police station. An hour and fifteen minutes later, "the fish-laden men walked into headquarters."

"Because of the cooperation given the police, one was released," the article says. "The other two posted $100 bonds on charges of petty larceny. In city court this week they failed to show."

KID MAGNET

Kids love Myrtle Beach, and while most visit with family and friends, some run away from home to get to the sand and sun. A few find jobs and stay. Others remain as long as their nest eggs hold out and then go home. A few break the law to get here and keep the momentum going once they arrive.

Harold Joseph Sladinger, "who claims he's 16 but is believed to be older," the *Sun News* reported in September 1962, was locked up in the Horry County jail. The article doesn't give the charges for which he was in jail, but it's noted that two weeks earlier, Sladinger, who was from Kinston, North Carolina, had "completed a 90-day term on the gang on charges of reckless driving, no driver's license and failure to yield the right-of-way."

He soon was behind bars again, and he made a plan to escape. The teenager asked his guard, Dayton Grainger, if he could make a phone call. Grainger let him out of the cell that Sladinger shared with four other inmates, and while he was locking the door Sladinger hit the guard over the head with a bar of soap in a sock. The jailer went to his knees, and the teen ran out the jail's back door.

Instead of leaving the area, Sladinger stole a pickup truck and drove to Surfside Beach. "He abandoned the truck and apparently spent Sunday on the beach in a 'borrowed' bathing suit," the article says, and then late on Sunday night, "Odessa Tarlton of Surfside heard her car start up and leave the driveway with the lights off."

She called the police, they gave chase, Sladinger wrecked Tarlton's car and the police took him back to jail.

UPROOTED

Locals joke about sharing the roads with tourists. We know to pause an extra second or two at intersections to make sure no one is running a red light, and we give a bit of extra space between cars because you never know when someone is going to zip across three lanes so they can turn in a beachwear store or all-you-care-to-eat buffet.

With so many out-of-town drivers gawking at their surroundings and trying to find their destinations, roadside landscaping sometimes suffers. The fall of 1962 was a rough season for palmetto trees that lined Kings Highway, the *Sun News* reported.

One palmetto was uprooted when a woman hit it, backed up and drove away. The palms suffered a double hit a few days later when a man, who was chasing his wife in another car, crashed his vehicle and took out two trees at Forty-sixth Avenue North.

That made five palmettos taken out by drivers within the first year of them being planted.

Not Ready to Leave

Many a parent who visits Myrtle Beach has heard when it's time to go home, "But I'm not ready to leave yet!"

Four teenage girls who visited Myrtle Beach over Easter weekend in April 1963 felt that way. The *Sun News* reported that two sisters and their two friends had stayed in a hotel with the sisters' parents, but when it was time to leave on Sunday, they didn't meet the adults at 1:00 p.m. at the Pavilion as was previously arranged. The girls went looking for boys.

At 5:00 p.m., when the girls still hadn't appeared, the parents went to the police. At seven o'clock that night, police officers found the two older girls, ages fifteen and sixteen, in a car with two boys from North Carolina, and they were returned to the parents. But the younger girls, both fourteen years old, were still missing, and by midnight, the entire police force was out looking for them.

On Monday afternoon, the two young teens were still missing, but police caught a break when a man reported he thought he saw them near a pier. The man said the girls told him they "weren't going home until their parents found them" and that they "had been on the beach for Easter but hadn't had a big enough blast yet."

Police officers found them on the beach a little after 5:00 p.m. Monday.

"The girls were reported in high spirits," the article says, "when they were found on the beach in the vicinity of the Ocean Plaza fishing pier at 5:10 p.m. Monday 'in the company of 6 or 7 boys and a good supply of beer.'"

Litter Crackdown

It would be a mistake to think litter is a minor problem in Myrtle Beach. When there are millions of vacationers leaving snack wrappers, cigarette butts, dirty diapers, drink cans, bottles, plastic bags, broken sun umbrellas and plastic shovels on the beaches, a critical situation arises that endangers the health, safety and quality of life for locals, visitors and wildlife.

Who picks up all the garbage? Within the city of Myrtle Beach, town employees pick up most of the discarded trash. In the days before the city had sand raking machines to sift out most of the debris, it was a backbreaking job. Trash became so overwhelming in 1963, Myrtle Beach police chief W.C. Newton asked the public to turn in litterers, and those found guilty could receive a fine of up to $100.

"If anyone sees violations of the ordinance, we ask that they get the license number of the car from which trash was thrown and report it to the police department."

There's no explanation of how an accused litterer could be proven guilty in those days before everyone had phone cameras in their pockets.

Litter is a major problem on public beaches, and local officials have been creative in dealing with it. *Photograph by Matt Silfer, Silfer Studios.*

BASE CRASHING

Base jumping, or jumping off a tall fixed object and parachuting to the ground, can be a fun sport in the right circumstances. While base jumping from the top of an oceanfront hotel might sound like a good idea—just land in the sand!—in reality oceanfront hotels are surrounded by other buildings and lots of cars and landscaping.

But in June 1988, twenty-eight-year-old Marlen Burford and twenty-four-year-old Steve Jester, both from Titusville, Florida, decided to base jump off the twenty-three-story Palace Resort. Jeter fell onto a car and a trash receptacle and "crashed through a wooden fence," according to an account in the Greenwood *Index-Journal*, but he walked away.

Burford wasn't so lucky. He "slammed into a seawall at the Landmark Best Western Resort Hotel" that was next door and "died of multiple injuries." His blood alcohol content made him legally intoxicated, the coroner said.

"It's a stupid sport," Jester said to the reporter. "We just pushed our odds too far. We just didn't think it could ever happen to us. I don't recommend anybody doing it."

Chapter 4

SPRING FLINGS

High school and college-age kids have been journeying to Myrtle Beach for spring break ever since students from Clemson and USC piled in Model Ts with a few jugs of moonshine. The tradition is as strong as ever, with Myrtle Beach landing third (out of twenty) on coed.com's 2015 list of Trashiest Spring Break Destinations.

College students come by the carload, bars and nightclubs fill up and the parties spill over into parking lots and beaches. Those younger than twenty-one who don't try to use fake IDs might rent houses with groups of friends, or the lucky ones have parents who own beach houses. These underage groups will often bring adult chaperones in whose names the houses are rented because many rental companies won't rent directly to teenagers.

It's not unusual for those teens to drink alcohol, often with the permission of the adults in the group, usually with the understanding that no one is to drive a car. It's considered by some a safe way to control inevitable partying.

Of course the hotels also fill up with high school and college students in April, May and June, and stories abound reporting drunk teens being messy, loud, rude, obnoxious and stupid. Sometimes reality television shows forge into the crowds and encourage ever more rowdy behavior with a focus on scantily clad young women. Alcohol companies flock to Myrtle Beach bars and hire plenty of sexy young women to draw in young men. They have special product promotions with attention-grabbing gimmicks like foam-daubing or black light parties.

The fun sometimes gets wild at spring break celebrations in Myrtle Beach. *Photograph by Matt Silfer, Silfer Studios.*

Girls just want to have fun during spring break at Myrtle Beach. *Photograph by Matt Silfer, Silfer Studios.*

With plenty of alcohol and drugs to fuel the parties, lapses in judgment are common. Myrtle Beach locals hope every year the students don't get hurt or hurt anyone else, but many years there are injuries and even tragic deaths, such as several times when young people have attempted to dive into hotel swimming pools from their balconies.

Here are a few stories from throughout the years that show why the Grand Strand is a hotbed of sizzling excitement and debauchery for students looking for release before and after year-end final exams.

HAD A GAS

The year 1966 marked a significant increase in spring break crowds in the Grand Strand area. That year, the number of visitors on Easter weekend was estimated between seventy-five and ninety thousand, with a little more than half of them college and high school students who mostly congregated in the Ocean Drive area of North Myrtle Beach.

That was also the year someone set off a tear gas bomb at the Pad, a dance spot popular with the college kids. Some three hundred students were in the building at the time, and another two hundred were outside.

"When the bomb exploded, the young people rushed toward a lattice wall, which they tore down in their efforts to escape," Ocean Drive police chief Merlin Bellamy was quoted as saying in the *Field & Herald*. "Our force was nearby and through a public address system talked to the youngsters in an attempt to prevent the spread of the incident. Some 12 to 13 persons were treated at the hospital and all released."

Despite the bomb and the large crowd, Bellamy said the number of arrests during the weekend was "surprisingly low."

As the years wore on, the parties became wilder.

OVERFLOWING JAILS

Spring break arrest numbers increased exponentially in the 1980s and '90s. It's interesting to note, however, that public officials often said to reporters, "It's not so bad," even when more than one thousand arrests were made in a single holiday weekend.

Whether a good time is too much fun is a matter of perception. *Photograph by Matt Silfer, Silfer Studios.*

That's what happened in 1989 when "more than 1,500 people were arrested on charges ranging from indecent exposure to public drunkenness along South Carolina's northern beaches over the Easter weekend," according to an Associated Press article in the Greenwood *Index-Journal*. Most of the arrests were alcohol related.

But police officers said, "There were no major incidents. 'On Saturday, there was more people down there…than I've ever seen,' North Myrtle Beach Police Chief Charles Sendler said. But, he added, 'it wasn't a bad weekend.'"

This relaxed public face in the aftermath of so many arrests is surprising, especially considering an article in the *Index-Journal* from one year earlier, in 1988. It says about 120 people younger than age twenty-one were arrested during Easter weekend, and the chief of enforcement for the Alcoholic Beverage Control Commission, Joe Dorton, said the number of arrests was "a little high. This really breaks down to about 60 arrests per night, and that's a little more than normal."

LINE IN THE SAND

A common point of contention in coastal tourist hot spots is between business owners and civic leaders. They debate where to draw the line between partying and breaking the law. It could mean the difference between riding a big wave of revenue or wiping out when the partyers take their wallets to a more accommodating beach town.

Business owners would like to curb theft, vandalism, breakage and other crimes, but they want the business spring breakers and other special events tourists bring. City leaders have to decide how much law enforcement is needed (within their means) to protect residents and visitors. It's nice to say that the problem could be solved with additional police presence, but budgets don't get balanced with all that overtime pay.

That balancing act was underlined in 1991 when "authorities in North Myrtle Beach cracked down on the spring break crowd over the Easter weekend, drawing complaints from college students and shop owners," according to an article in the Gaffney *Ledger*.

The *Ledger* reported that 267 arrests were made for underage drinking compared to 64 the year before. The director of public safety reported to North Myrtle Beach town council members that, probably not coincidentally, there were ten fewer traffic accidents and four fewer fire department responses.

The president of the North Strand Ministerial Alliance, Preston Huntley, was pleased with the crackdown and said, "Easter is the holiest time in our lives. I appreciate city council's efforts."

However, many students vowed to never return to North Myrtle Beach, and business owners were displeased with fewer sales. A restaurateur said his sub shop's revenue was reduced by a third, and a motel owner said "his business suffered considerably."

The article ended with several paragraphs about how retailers in Daytona Beach, Florida, would welcome the disgruntled students, and that Daytona "last year had 400,000 visitors during six weeks from March through April."

In 1995, Myrtle Beach hired additional police officers to patrol Ocean Boulevard during spring break, and they made two thousand more misdemeanor arrests than the previous year and almost doubled the amount of fines it collected, from $310,965 in 1994 to $601,215 in 1995. Most of the additional fine income, the *Index-Journal* reported, would be used to cover the additional law enforcement expenses.

In that case, the article said, "Ocean Boulevard merchants have repeatedly called for more police in their area, the district near the Myrtle Beach Pavilion Amusement Park."

Plenty of high school and college-age spring breakers still visit the Myrtle Beach area, and there are still plenty of stupid and silly incidents, but law enforcement methods have adapted to defuse potential alcohol-fueled mobs and to more strictly enforce laws prohibiting underage drinking.

Spring Bike Rallies

Two other "spring flings" in the Myrtle Beach area are when bikers rally in the Grand Strand area. One event spans the second and third weekends in May while the other is held on Memorial Day weekend.

Through the years, the two May rallies had attendance swell into the hundreds of thousands, and eventually, the second rally outnumbered the first. The first rally was and is composed of mostly white Harley bikers ages twenty-five to sixty. The second rally has historically been mostly African American street bikers ages twenty to sixty, with a high number in the twenty to thirty-five age range. However, both rallies include people of all races and ages and don't discriminate. At the rallies, anyone on a motorcycle is just another biker.

As the rallies have grown, so has their rambunctiousness. In the 1990s and 2000s, the first May rally became notorious for activities such as "weenie bite" contests, in which women stand up on the back pegs and try to bite a hot dog on a string; increasingly suggestive clothing, including body paint instead of clothing or moments of females going topless; drag racing; tire burnouts; excessive revving; driving under the influence; fights; and other crimes. Reports in the media about biker groups such as Hells Angels coming to possibly spread mayhem made many residents uneasy.

The second May rally has its epicenter at the tiny municipality of Atlantic Beach, which is a few blocks within the city of North Myrtle Beach. Also known as the Black Pearl, it was the only beach along the Grand Strand where blacks were welcome before integration. This rally became increasingly stressful for some locals as female bikers wore thong bikinis and riders sped and passed traffic by splitting lanes. Groups of bikers, along with thousands of people driving souped-up cars, impeded the flow of traffic. Traffic was often at a standstill on U.S. 17 and other areas during the peak Memorial

Day weekend rally. The expense of three hundred additional police officers and post-rally cleanups became an increasing civic burden.

Tensions reached crescendos in 2008 and 2009. In May 2008, during the second rally, a local twenty-year-old college student was shot and killed by a local teenager during a dispute over a parking spot. In September 2008, the Myrtle Beach City Council passed fifteen new ordinances that declared "unpermitted events and rallies to be public nuisances"; restricted the hours of operation for businesses that serve beer and wine and allow "drinking contests or games, or contests involving disrobing, or 'wet t-shirt', 'Girls Gone Wild' or similar contests"; put restrictions on the sound level that could be emitted from motorcycles; and put in place a citywide helmet law (which was later struck down).

In 2009, the two May motorcycle rallies were still held from May 8 to 17 and May 21 to 25, but official events were planned outside Myrtle Beach city limits, such as in Murrells Inlet and North Myrtle Beach. Attendance numbers were down.

On May 22, 2011, following the first spring rally, *Sun News* reporter Tonya Root wrote, "Vendors, visitors and residents said this year's rally increased in size and attendance, but it was not close to the rally's heyday of several years ago when as many as 500,000 people attended. They estimated between 75,000 and 100,000 people were in town for this year's rally."

For many bikers, actions by public officials since 2008 changed the tone and appeal of the rallies, at least within the city of Myrtle Beach. The first May biker rally now has its main activity hubs located north, west and south of the Myrtle Beach City limits, although some Myrtle Beach businesses book entertainment during rally dates.

As for the second May bike rally, the tiny municipality of Atlantic Beach cannot provide accommodations for the thousands upon thousands of attendees. In 2014, a good number of them stayed in Myrtle Beach, and at one point, the crowd surged into a main north–south thoroughfare and took over the street. All weekend, homeowners and business owners in the downtown area reported fights, theft, being threatened with guns, people urinating in public, tire slashings and more.

On the Saturday night of that holiday weekend, five people were shot and three killed in Myrtle Beach hotels. The next week, outraged citizens filled a city council meeting and took turns airing their grievances. They insisted that something be done to curb the lawlessness and violence.

In 2014 and early 2015, Myrtle Beach City and Horry County officials worked together with law enforcement agencies to make plans for a safer

Memorial Day weekend that included millions in funding for new police equipment, additional law enforcement officers, road barricades and a plan for a traffic loop designed to keep vehicles and people moving.

Chapter 5

BOOTLEGGING AND OTHER DRINKING STORIES

While it's hard to pin down how much of a role fermented beverages played in the lives of Native Americans, there's ample documentation showing that European colonists brought their firmly entrenched drinking habits with them.

The area around Georgetown had many well-to-do families, including fabulously wealthy indigo and rice plantation owners. They generally had their big meals around 2:00 p.m., and those included wines and cordials. As the eighteenth century merged into the nineteenth, rum punch was a favorite drink of the elite in addition to gin, wines, fruit brandies like plum and raspberry, fruity persimmon beer and spruce beer. President George Washington, who visited the Grand Strand in 1791, was fond of rum punch, beer, hard cider, porter and wines, especially Madeira. He had his own rye whiskey distillery at Mount Vernon.

As time went on, people opposed to alcohol became more vocal. In the mid-1800s, temperance societies gained popularity and members. Those groups were religious in foundation, and in 1886, something happened that seemed to prove a point for people who abstained on religious grounds.

A SIGN FROM GOD

The earthquake of August 31, 1886, that devastated Charleston also affected Horry County, and one of its repercussions was that many people thought it was a punishment from God for their sins, including growing grapevines and making wine.

Noah W. Cooper wrote an account of the earthquake experienced in the Cool Spring area that was published in April 1951 in the *Mullins Enterprise* and republished by the Horry County Historical Society. Cooper said he was awakened about 10:00 p.m. by a "terrible noise."

> *The house seemed to be breaking up. It was cracking and twisting and moving up and down. The noise sounded like the earth bellowing in mighty pain…Another great roar like thunder underground and a movement of the earth made us dumb with fear. We ran out on the ground. The oaks in the yard were swaying back and forth although there was no wind. I feared that the earth would open up and swallow us. We huddled together till the great roar subsided.*

Aftershocks filled Cooper and his housemates with fresh terror, and he described a "mighty thundering sound and a roar from underground." As the tremors continued, the neighborhood began to be filled with the sounds of residents crying and praying. One of the voices he heard crying to God came from Bill Mishoe, who lived a mile away. Cooper walked to Mishoe's house.

> *The air along the way was full of fearful cries and prayers to God for forgiveness and for safety. I never heard such agony and earnest pleas to Heaven. Occasionally a tremor would come so strong and violent that I would stop and catch hold to a bush. And I myself prayed as I had always been taught to pray. I found Bill on his knees near the front gate of the house where he lived with his wife and mother-in-law. He was praying very loud and sweat was pouring from his face. His mother-in-law was sitting in the middle of the yard in an old rocking chair praying aloud but without fear. She was saying, "Oh, Mr. Cooper, the world is coming to an end. God is disgusted with the wickedness of the people. I am not afraid. I am ready to go, and I expect the world to be ended before daylight. I'm going home. Glory to God! Hallelujah!"*

Bill Mishoe finally calmed down after Cooper explained it was an earthquake, but the mother-in-law continued rocking and "telling us that in a few hours she would see God." Cooper walked back to his home in the early morning and said the tremors continued until dawn.

After strong ones, he heard his neighbors' "prayers and cries increased in loudness and intenseness."

After breakfast, Cooper headed to the schoolhouse where many frightened people were gathered. As he explained what he knew of the history of earthquakes and how people in flat rural areas such as western Horry County weren't usually killed by them, "there came a mighty roar like thunder from underground and in the air, and the whole earth began to shake under us and the trees to waver."

The schoolhouse shook, and its chimney tumbled down. "A field of cotton nearby waved and moved up and down as if it were on a boat in a storm at sea," Cooper wrote and added, "Tremors continued with more or less violence for over a month." The Sunday following the great earthquake, churches were full, and "most preachers told their audiences that the earthquake was just a reminder that God was disgusted with their sinful conduct and that they had best turn from their evil way, pray more and be righteous in their conduct."

Many preachers recommended ceasing making and drinking wine and advised people to cut down their grapevines.

"Nearly everybody in those days made their own wine and cider, or they were in easy reach of those wanting them, until the year of the earthquake when many became so frightened at what they considered a terrible visitation of an angry God on account of the sins of the people and resolved to turn from the error of their way and allowed their vines to fall down and forsook their cider presses," read a history column in the November 4, 1909 issue of the *Horry Herald*. "These liquids were scarce the year after that event and neither love nor money could purchase them except on rare occasions."

Temperance societies gained more members than ever after the earthquake, but it was hard for all Grand Stranders to completely give up alcohol. Through colonization, the Revolutionary War, the Civil War and both world wars, South Carolinians have made corn liquor and other less potent alcoholic beverages like fruit beers, brandies and wines. Coastal residents may not have as much notoriety for liquor stills as their mountain dwelling brethren, but liquor production wasn't unusual. In the late 1800s, people in the Conway area could give their mailman a corn whiskey order and some cash, and the next day's mail brought the goods. Occasionally a bottle broke, and the mail was saturated.

Back in those days, it was common for a bowl of spiked punch to be found on family tables with a communal dipper for anyone to take refreshment. Many men kept flasks handy for when they met their neighbors on the road or at social events. Sharing a nip was a form of how-do-you-do with the added element of wanting to brew, as a point of pride, the finest liquor in the neighborhood.

"It was a salute, a salutation, that every man carried a flask in his pocket," Walter Hill, director of the Horry County Museum, said in January 2015. "When you were riding down the road or walking down the road and you'd see your neighbor, you'd say, 'Hey, how you doin'? Would you like a drink?'…and you stopped right there…If you pulled up there hunting or if you pulled up there to the store or something and there was a crowd of men around there and everybody there spoke [to you], you pulled that bottle out and you took the lid off and bump, bump, bump, bump, then you put the lid back on and put it back in there…It was just a salutation. Everybody shared a drink. It was a social thing."

Prohibition

During Prohibition (1919–33), "rumrunners found the islands and inlets of the [Grand Strand] as attractive as the earlier pirates and later drug runners," Catherine Lewis wrote for the *Independent Republic Quarterly*.

> *Older citizens will sometimes talk of the big black cars and the strange city types who came to Little River in those days. One story tells about a large ship anchored offshore at White Point, south of Windy Hill Beach, in deep water. Small boats brought the cargo to the strand. Boards were laid down for the truck wheels to run on. After the transfer the strand and the dirt in the woods were swept to blot out the trucks or evidence. Federal agents arrested the man on whose land the ship was unloading and picked up other little people, mostly local, who were involved, but did not snare any of the big operators. When these locals were brought before a federal jury consisting of other locals, they were turned loose out of a sense of fundamental fairness.*

In 1932, some bootleggers were spectacularly unlucky, John P. Cartrette reported in the October 1975 issue of the *Independent Republic Quarterly*, when they sent a telegram from Florence to people up north saying, "We have the baby. What shall we do with it?" This was their code phrase to let folks know that a whiskey shipment arrived. However, the message was sent shortly after American aviator Charles Lindbergh's baby was kidnapped.

The FBI swooped down, shot it out and arrested some parties camped on a farm at the edge of Timmonsville, S.C. They shot it out with a car on the highway near there and seized a truck load of whiskey at the edge of Conway, one at Marion, and two or three in Georgetown and Florence counties. At White Point, south of Windy Hill Beach, they arrested the man on whose land the ship was unloading. The large ship anchored offshore in deep water, and small boats brought the cargo to the strand.

Most local churches did not condone drinking alcohol, and many members were not afraid to call the law on their own parishioners, especially if they showed up drunk for services. An article in the May 2, 1946 edition of the *Horry Herald* has a front-page headline that reads, "Shows a Disregard Laws and Religion" and names several people who were intoxicated on church grounds, among other offenses such as resisting arrest, carrying a concealed weapon and disturbing a religious worship. After a lecture from the judge, they were each fined twenty-seven dollars and warned that if it happened again they'd spend time on the county chain gang.

Taxing Times

Making corn liquor became more complicated after the Civil War because the federal government decided to start taxing it to pay war debts. That didn't sit well with southerners, and that's when the revenue men, or revenuers, started hunting down and busting up stills that sold their products without being registered to pay taxes. These were often large stills that produced many gallons at a time.

Especially during Prohibition, Horry County Museum director Walter Hill said, small stills used on top of woodstoves were popular for home use. Sold in local hardware stores and marketed as perfume or medicinal distilleries, they could produce only enough liquor for one family, so they didn't attract notice from tax collectors. If you didn't want to make your own beverages, it wasn't hard to find some to buy. Lillian Mills* remembers a popular bootleg liquor spot.

When she was growing up in the 1930s and '40s there was a "little long house that was like a shotgun house where the Lutheran church is there just at North Myrtle Beach, by the cemetery." In that building, she said, was a "man who lived there [who] sold bootleg liquor." Everyone knew it, she

During Prohibition, miniature stovetop stills like this one on display at the Horry County Museum were sold at hardware stores as "perfume distilleries." *Photograph by Matt Silfer, Silfer Studios.*

said, but she doesn't recall him ever being arrested. "If you wanted some moonshine, you'd just go to his house, and he'd have it for you" in either pint- or quart-size Mason jars.

The South Carolina coast was particularly wet with alcohol during Prohibition because there was a steady supply from local stills and from ships and boats dropping off supplies at coastal ports and river docks.

Powell Fisher, who used to own Oliver's Lodge restaurant in Murrells Inlet, told the story about brothers Ben and Bill McCoy. The men were boat builders from Halifax County, Florida, and during Prohibition, Bill became a bootlegger who ran shipments of high-quality rum and Scotch whisky between Florida, the Bahamas, Scotland and New York City.

The story goes that the brothers often stopped in Murrells Inlet, and Bill's fishing schooner, the *Arethusa*, was hidden near where Rum Gully Road is, in the Mount Gilead subdivision. The brothers earned reputations for their undiluted liquor, and those premium bottles became known as the "Real McCoys." To this day, Daytona Beach has an annual Real McCoy Rum Festival.

An *Horry Herald* article dated September 6, 1923, is from the middle of the Prohibition years. Its headline is "Bootlegger Is Caught at Game."

> *Melvin Causee was arrested near Myrtle Beach on Saturday before last while violating the prohibition laws. The arrest was made by D.F. Bellamy of the county rural police.*
>
> *Causee had his supply about a mile from the beach and kept it hid behind some gallberry bushes* [a small evergreen holly also known as an inkberry bush]. *He would go down to the strand and round the hotel and yacht club until he made up a batch of buyers to suit his taste, then he would take them over to the gallberry bush and dish out the juice in any quantity demanded. The policeman got on to his game and played hide and seek with him for a brief time until he had the proof of his violation of the law. The man was lodged in the jail here on Saturday night.*

POST-PROHIBITION STILLS

Producing off-the-grid corn liquor remained a popular business even after the end of Prohibition in 1933. Newspapers from the 1930s through the 1960s are dotted with articles about lawmen hunting down stills, like a one-paragraph item in the June 30, 1949 issue of the *Horry Herald*. Four police officers "were in the Jamb section a few days ago and captured a copper still and 900 gallons of sour mash at a location back of Toney Grainger's. The still was of 100 gallon capacity. No arrest has yet been made in connection with this still."

In October 1950, the *Tabor City Tribune* ran an article datelined in Conway and headlined "Liquor Still Captured by Deputy Bell."

Conway—Horry County law enforcement officers, cracking down on lawlessness in Horry County, raided a liquor still six miles out of Conway on old highway 501, Tuesday morning and captured a 200 gallon still and 10 barrels of mash…The raid took place Tuesday morning at 11:30. Eugene Mitchell and Billy Chestnut, who strolled into the still unaware that it had been raided were arrested and admitted operating the still. Two other operators who escaped are still at large.

A little later that same month, the paper reported several more Horry County raids:

Sheriff's officers made a number of raids on illicit whiskey dealers within the last few days among them the following:

On Thursday of last week Officers H.M. Allen, J.E. Jordan, DeVon Bell and W.C. Carter made a raid at the place of E.M. Soles located on No. 9, near Nixon's Cross Roads. At that place they confiscated a lot of contraband liquor and a quantity of beer that had not paid any license.

The same officers made a raid on a place operated by Lottie Ward in what is called Ward Town, not far from Ocean Drive. A lot of contraband whiskey was taken and confiscated.

On last Friday night a raid was made at Bill Barringer's by Deputy Sheriffs Lee Johnson and H.M. Allen. A quantity of liquor was confiscated and taken in the place.

On last Monday a liquor still which had evidently been operating unlawfully was captured and broken up and destroyed. This still was located two miles from the Coffee Pot on the Myrtle Beach highway and was hidden off about 300 yards from the highway. This still had been watched for sometime in an effort to catch the operator of it which failed. The officers catching the still were: H.M. Allen, J.E. Jordan, Calhoun and Lewis.

The violators were all put under bonds for trial at court except in the case of the captured still.

Bootlegging thrived in 1951. On May 31, the *Field* reported several arrests, starting with a man caught when officers, who were engaged in breaking up a still, heard a noise. They looked around and found James Leonard in a fifteen-foot-deep well that he had been digging for the liquor operation. He was hauled out and arrested.

In the same article, it was reported that Johnny Edwards was arrested after officers destroyed his 1,300 gallons of mash and confiscated two cases of liquor; and a copper still in the Jamb section of Horry County that had 100 gallons of mash was destroyed.

Also in May 1951, Ernest Todd, who lived on the farm of Jim Tompkins, reacted to police officers coming in the door by throwing a bucket of liquor in one of their faces. "A sufficient amount was saved to verify the fact that it was corn liquor," the article says.

In January 1952, creative measures were taken to make an arrest. Officers heard a certain female bootlegger pour her whiskey down the kitchen drain when she saw the law coming. The next time they visited, an officer sneaked over to the end of her drainpipe, which was out in the yard, and caught the evidence.

Distribution was also creative. A service station in the Green Sea area of Horry County was raided in 1953, and fifty-six half-pints of whiskey were confiscated from an operating vending machine.

In 1955, Horry County deputy sheriff Ernest Stroud was driving in the Cedar Creek section of the county up near Little River when he noticed an unusually large number of cars parked in the yard of a "little white and green cottage," the *Florence Morning News* reported. It turned out the one-room cottage was shielding from view a newly built "packhouse" that contained mash vats, boilers and stills.

"The bootleggers used a large blower to get rid of smoke and the smell," the article says. "They used a septic tank for the waste mash and used chemicals to destroy the odor…An electric bell was rigged to the back of the stove in the packhouse to warn of anyone approaching the operation. In case a raid might be staged, the bootleggers had a trap door built at the back so that they could escape to the woods. The door was hardly noticeable from the outside."

Although the sheriff's department conducted a raid, the place was empty when they arrived. The operation was described as "the largest liquor still ever to operate in Horry County."

Illegal liquor sales were so common that sometimes law enforcement officers stumbled upon booze. In 1963, a policeman in Atlantic Beach went into a club looking for a stolen radio. Instead, he discovered a trapdoor under the refrigerator, where a cache held nine half-gallon containers of corn whiskey, "plus assorted half-pints of stamped liquor."

THIRST QUENCHING

In 1973, it became legal for bars and restaurants to purchase permits allowing them to sell beer, wine and cocktails. Before then, people "brown bagged"—brought their own liquor to bars and restaurants—and then paid premium fees for setups of mixers and ice.

Although it was several more years before any type of alcohol, including beer and wine, could be legally sold on Sundays, locals found their ways around the laws.

Jack Thompson, who is acknowledged as the premier Myrtle Beach photo-historian, was a customer at the Tom Davis Trailer Park off Ninth Avenue South. At the entrance was a ramshackle convenience store where just about everything from food to firewood was sold. Just inside the door, Davis could be found "snoozing" in a hammock. He didn't mind if someone came in the store on Sundays, grabbed a six-pack and left the money on the counter.

Tawny Monroe* remembers how at the Roma restaurant in Myrtle Beach, customers came in on Sundays and ordered "the special coffee." It was actually red wine served in opaque mugs.

In 1991, Myrtle Beach bars and restaurants could finally sell alcohol on Sundays (North Myrtle Beach approved Sunday cocktails in 1985), but it was 2003 before beer and wine could be sold on Sundays at Horry and Georgetown Counties' convenience and grocery stores.

Before the start of 2006, the Myrtle Beach area was known as the tourist destination serving the strongest drinks in the country because until then South Carolina bars and restaurants could make cocktails with only 1.7-ounce mini bottles, such as the ones served on airplanes. Many people who didn't want such strong drinks requested their beverages be "split" or "split two ways" so that the mini bottle was divided between two drinks. The late Tom Sponseller, who was the president of the South Carolina Hospitality Association in 2006, said in a *USA Today* article that sixty to seventy million mini bottles were sold annually in South Carolina before liquor by the drink was approved. Doing away with mini bottles made the drinks a little weaker and their prices lower.

At first, local bar and restaurant owners grumbled about the need for more shelf space for large liquor bottles and the trouble of developing an inventory system to keep track of liquor by the drink, but they soon adapted.

As of 2015, restaurants and bars can serve alcohol every day, including Sundays, if they pay for the permit. Bottles of liquor (like whiskey or vodka) can be sold only in Alcohol Beverage Control (ABC) stores, and they aren't open on Sundays. Horry County grocery stores and convenience stores can sell beer and wine 24/7.

Chapter 6
SEXY SEVENTIES AND EROTIC EIGHTIES

Myrtle Beach has been known as a magnet for hearty partiers since the early 1900s when the first shoe tapped on the Pavilion dance floor. But those revelers aren't just visitors: Grand Strand locals are infamous for knowing how to have good times. Through Prohibition, after World War II and into the 1950s and '60s, Myrtle Beach was the place to be along the South Carolina coast for sun worshiping and dancing, as well as gambling, drinking and/or drugging.

In the 1970s and '80s, the partying took on a high-rolling frenzy when disco queens, cocaine and Quaaludes were mixed with high-stakes sports gambling.

THE DISCO ERA

Tawny Monroe* grew up in Myrtle Beach, and she got into the nightlife scene starting at a young age in the early 1970s.

"I was going to the Hop 'n' Hutch at thirteen," she said in September 2014, "and didn't pay for a drink ever in my entire life. The Hop 'n' Hutch was a bar for young teenagers."

In those days, Monroe said, U.S. 17 Bypass was red clay, and the young teens had campouts along the Intracoastal Waterway. They were careful in North Myrtle Beach because the police were strict, "but Myrtle Beach—cross the line and you could do whatever you want[ed]."

In the late 1970s, Tramps was a popular disco in the Windy Hill section of North Myrtle Beach. *Author's collection.*

As in years past, when the South Carolina coast provided an easy avenue for bootleggers to import alcohol by boat, in the 1970s and '80s, there was a brisk illegal drug market with shipments straight from Colombia.

"We used to smoke pot in Chapin Park—all the young people did," Monroe, now a well-to-do grandmother, said. "We smoked pot every single day. We did Quaaludes, drank. Nobody thought anything of drinking and driving then."

By the time Monroe was sixteen years old, the disco era was in full Hustle mode, and popular clubs included the Colony and Tramps. Both had backgammon rooms where people could take breaks from the dance floor and get a bite to eat.

Tramps was in the Windy Hill section of North Myrtle Beach, and Monroe remembers it had murals of old movie stars, such as Humphrey Bogart and Lauren Bacall, along with memorabilia from the Ocean Forest Hotel, which was demolished in 1974. It had two bars—one at the front, where a big group of local girls liked to hang out, and another farther back, where tourists were directed to go. The dance floor was stainless steel, and the ceiling flashed colored lights. Live entertainment included many disco stars of the day, including Sister Sledge, and a burlesque show for the ladies called the Peter Adonis Male Traveling Fantasy Show.

"Tramps Dancing Backgammon Club," an advertisement in the April 9–15, 1978 issue of *Coast* magazine says. "A Little Intimate, A Little Wild! Come to Tramps for an exotic Piña Colada, Hurricane, Tijuana Cherry, Cotton Tail and Frozen Daiquiri. The Paradise Café Featuring Kosher Sandwiches, Steaks and Appetizers."

Richard Williams* also patronized Tramps and recalls unbridled sexuality.

"You would stand there with your back to the bar at Tramps," he said, "never facing the bartender. People would come over and put their hands on you, and you could put your hands on them…but you need to talk to Chip White. Chip was their impresario at Tramps."

Chip White grew up in North Myrtle Beach and says he was a regular at Tramps beginning at the club's opening night in the mid-1970s, when he was about fifteen or sixteen years old.

"When Tramps started, I was completely underage," he said, "but I had a fake ID. I was always going in, but for the first several years it was there, I wasn't even legal."

White was known as a sharp dresser and smooth dancer. Everyone dressed up to go out in those days.

"There was a period one summer where I either wore white pants or black pants," he said. "We had those below-the-knee boots that zipped up, and you'd tuck your pants into them. We had the shirt unbuttoned down to the navel, tight pants, bell-bottoms, flared. Toward the end you'd try to find pleated pants, unconstructed blazers."

White described evenings that began at 9:00 or 10:00 p.m. and ended six or seven hours later after much dancing, drinking and drugs. He remembers inhaling "poppers"—butyl or amyl nitrite—at a song's peak, to get an intense euphoric rush that lasted about thirty seconds.

"The first time I ever did coke was on my way to Tramps," he said, "and the second time was in the bathroom at Tramps—that same night. We definitely did a ton of coke there. And Quaaludes. It was the sex, drug and disco era for us."

A particularly memorable night, White said, was when his sister, *Wheel of Fortune* star Vanna White, had a friend who owned a Rolls Royce. They drove it to Tramps with Chip in the back seat and were allowed to park it in front of the club, under its canopy.

DEEP POCKETS AND GOOD STUFF IN 'EM

Another nightclub open in the disco era was the Colony, which was more exclusive than Tramps. It was at the north end of Myrtle Beach, on Restaurant Row across from the former Cagney's restaurant.

The late-night atmosphere was hedonistic.

"Everybody did Quaaludes, smoked pot, drank liquor, danced to disco music," Tawny Monroe said. "We had sex in the bar, blowjobs in the bathrooms, girls making out under the piano. We were wearing see-through dresses and nothing underneath, platform [shoes]. We did amyl nitrite on the dance floor, and everything was in the open, too. We did coke out in the open, pretty much…There were many discos here, and it was just craziness. Drugs. Everybody was bisexual. Nobody knew about AIDS yet. It wasn't until 1979–80 that we started hearing about it. Homosexuality, bisexuality, open sex, threesomes, drug use. It was crazy. It was wild here in Myrtle Beach."

The Colony wasn't open long enough for Chip White to experience it as an adult, but his mother took him there when he was a teenager.

"That was a wild place," he said. "It sounded wilder than it was. The legends are bigger than the place, but it was fun. Those were some crazy times."

Richard Williams*, who is a few years older than White, was a regular at the Colony.

If you weren't a local, or a shaker and a mover, you didn't get into the Colony. You didn't go to the Colony unless you looked really good. You didn't get in unless you were really good. It was our Studio 54.

It had wonderful furniture, a great bar. There was a very nice, fancy, backgammon room off to the right, and on occasion, there was a backroom where there was a little blackjack played…It had good security. It was the place where it was fine if the girls danced together, but the boys didn't dance together. The lights would go out at times on purpose for certain spots. Everyone had a really bad sinus drainage issue during the Colony.

The Colony was fabulous, just fabulous. You went to the Colony to have a really good time with the locals. It was wide fucking open. And you can quote me on that—wide fucking open. It did not matter what you did there, no one said. And you would see things. No nakedness or lasciviousness, but…everyone was extremely comfortable there. Nobody made any judgments.

Williams recalls a Halloween party that is now regarded as the apex of the Colony's decadent reputation. The club's owner, dressed in an extremely revealing Elvira costume, greeted guests while in a coffin. One couple, dressed as King Neptune and his female consort, wore only green-dyed fishnet and glitter.

"You would go from the Colony to the Afterdeck," Williams said. "People would just be handing out Quaaludes and saying, 'Oh here, have one of these. Do you want to go outside? If you want a line, go with me. Come to my car for a minute.'"

A party all the movers and shakers wanted to attend in 1978 was the opening of the USS *Sequoia*, a former U.S. presidential yacht that was open to the public for two seasons as a tourist attraction at Vereen's Marina in North Myrtle Beach. One couple in attendance was John and Rita Jenrette. John was a U.S. congressman from Myrtle Beach, and he was two years away from being caught accepting a $50,000 bribe in a federal sting known as the Abscam operation. He was later tried and convicted.

Rita was young and beautiful, and she became infamous for saying she and John had sex on the U.S. Capitol steps. It was a claim she later retracted.

Rita described her life during that period in an autobiographical article she co-wrote for the April 1981 issue of *Playboy* magazine.

> *At first, I desperately wanted to be accepted. But I failed to appreciate the fact that appearances are everything in Washington. I was naïve enough, or stubborn enough, to think I could wear my gypsy outfit, speak frankly and still win out over my detractors. Too flashy, too blonde, too outspoken, they said. I was ten points down before I knew it. For five years, though, I gave it my best shot. I shook hands in the Bi-Lo shopping center parking lot, hit tennis balls during American Cancer Society benefits, helped write my husband's speeches, licked fund-raising envelopes and attended Rotary Club testimonials, greased pig contests and church suppers. And I struggled to keep his career together as his drinking grew worse, even as some of his political supporters gossiped that I was a gold digger who had married John for his position.*

Jennifer New* of North Myrtle Beach attended the June 1978 pre-opening party on the USS *Sequoia*, and more than thirty years later, it was easy for her to recall Rita Jenrette. "It was like five o'clock. All the women were there in sundresses," New said, "and I turn around and there was a woman right behind me who had blue eye shadow up to here, as much blue eye shadow as was ever made in the world. She had a black knit-type dress cut down to here and up to here. It was Rita. She was trashy. So totally out of place."

*article By RITA JENRETTE
with KATHLEEN MAXA*

The Liberation
of a
Congressional Wife

*since the abscam scandal derailed her husband's political career
and her marriage headed for the rocks,
rita jenrette has emerged with a mission of her own*

I NEVER looked like a Congressman's wife. Instead of wearing tailored gabardine suits and sensible pumps, I favored silky—some said clinging—dresses and high-heeled boots. I preferred mink to camel's hair. My blonde hair had never been shaped into one of those sculptured coiffures favored by well-turned-out Washington matrons. At the Congressional wives' luncheon for Mrs. Anwar Sadat, I was the only one in a gypsy outfit.

Five years ago, when I married John Wilson Jenrette, Democratic Congressman from South Carolina, I was 26, closer in age to his junior staffers than to the wives of his colleagues. As a result, I was often mistaken for his mistress or his secretary at political gatherings we attended together. Once, at a Capitol Hill reception honoring nurses attending a convention, a nurse pressed her hotel key into John's hand, apparently oblivious of me standing at his side. "You're the best-looking thing I've seen all day," she told my husband. And Strom Thurmond, the senior Senator from John's home state, never did bother to learn my name. Meeting me, he'd turn to my husband and say, "Well, John, every time I see you, you're with a pretty little blonde."

I didn't fit the small-town Southern definition of a political wife any better. One well-meaning Myrtle Beach, South Carolina, matron took me aside shortly after I married John to advise me: "Now that you're a Congressman's wife, you have to look like one." Partly out of insecurity, partly out of curiosity, I submitted to her makeover. That night, I made my political debut in the Sixth Congressional District looking like a stand-in for Laverne or Shirley, with a beehive hairdo and Cleopatra-style eye make-up. Rather than offend the woman, I grinned and bore it.

Now, as I look back on my life as Mrs. Congressman Jenrette, I realize that long before my husband was convicted of bribery and conspiracy last October in an ABSCAM case, I had, by Washington political standards, already been found guilty of an equally serious offense: not fitting in.

At first, I desperately wanted to be accepted. But I failed to appreciate the fact that appearances are everything in Washington. I was naïve enough, or stubborn enough, to think I could wear my gypsy outfit, speak frankly and still win out over my detractors. Too flashy, too blonde, too outspoken, they said. I was ten points

When the photo above was taken on a California beach the day after John Jenrette's resignation from Congress, Rita still believed she could save their marriage. The couple has since separated and she's seeking an independent career.

PHOTOGRAPHY BY POMPEO POSAR/PRODUCED BY JEFF COHEN

Rita Jenrette, wife of South Carolina congressman John Jenrette, wrote an article that was published with semi-nude photographs in the April 1981 issue of *Playboy* magazine. *Author's collection.*

Also in June 1978, the Rolling Stones performed at the Myrtle Beach Convention Center. Promoter Cecil Corbett, a local, and his associates brought the Stones to Myrtle Beach as part of the band's desire to play small venues and connect more intimately with their fans. Tickets went for ten dollars each, each person could buy only two (in person, at the convention center box office) and there were 2,200 tickets up for grabs. They sold out in less than two hours.

"It was just like having your own private concert," Richard Williams said. "The events afterward were quite interesting…Cecil Corbett and that crowd—they had deep pockets and good stuff in 'em is what they always said."

One of the Stones concert organizers owed Tawny Monroe a favor, and she cashed it in on a pair of "front row center" seats. The national notoriety gained from the Stones visiting Myrtle Beach, which was big news, intensified the partying for a long while.

Part of the money fueling the partying came from gambling.

Chapter 7

"PUT THE BET DOWN"

G ambling has long provided backroom entertainment at Myrtle Beach establishments, but most forms of it have not been legal in South Carolina since the late nineteenth century. That hasn't stopped entrepreneurs from trying to get around the laws.

One of the earliest gambling venues was Washington Park Horse Race Track, which was located on what was later the site of Myrtle Square Mall and is now an empty lot between Kings Highway and Oak Street. It operated from 1938 through 1947 and was an "elaborate racing complex" that "included a half-mile track, stables for 150 horses, and semi-weekly races with an average $250 purse," the Myrtle Beach Comprehensive Plan says.

But there was a problem: Parimutuel betting was illegal in South Carolina. To get around that, Myrtle Beach city leaders passed a law that allowed racetrack betting by describing it as a form of entertainment. They said it was "guessing," not betting. A court case attempting to ban this "parimutuel guessing" went all the way to the South Carolina Supreme Court before state law was upheld, and the horse racetrack, along with a dog-racing track, had to close.

Many locals recount stories of backroom poker and blackjack tables in restaurants and bars. Historian and journalist Frank Beacham tells how Charlie Fitzgerald, who owned a black nightclub called Charlie's Place in Myrtle Beach in the 1940s and '50s, liked to play Georgia Skin in a private room.

In 1939, novelist and folklorist Zora Neale Hurston explained in a Works Progress Administration interview how Georgia Skin was played.

That's the most favorite gambling game among the workers of the South, and they lose money on the drop of a card, the fall of a card. And there's a rhythm to the fall of a card. And after they get set with the two principles, and the other people are called pikers, and anybody that wants a special card, he pick it out and he call that "picking one in the rough." They take a deck of cards and they shuffle it real good, and watch the man to be sure he don't steal nothing; that is that he don't set a card. There are four cards of every kind in the deck. And when a card [falls] like the card you have selected for, you lose. Sometimes when you don't watch the dealer he'll shuffle three cards just like his own down to the bottom of the deck so everybody falls before he does, and then he wins all the money. He puts [the deck] on the table; they don't allow him to hold it because they're afraid he'll steal. He puts in on the table and he turns off a card. Card by card. And the cards that's just like yours, when it falls you lose. And so they holler when he gets all set, when the principles have got their cards and all the pikers have got theirs and then the man will say, "Want'em to put the bet down." Then they'll say, "Put the money on the wood and make the bet go good." And then again, "Put it in sight and save a fight." And so they'll all get their bets down and they'll holler, "Let the deal go down. Boys, let the deal go down." And some of them will start singing.

In October 1951, FBI agents seized a dozen "digger" types of gambling devices. We know them today as crane games: you drop in a coin or token, and you have a few seconds to try to maneuver a hinged crane to a spot where it picks up a prize and then drops it into a slot where it can be retrieved. The machines were found at a Myrtle Beach warehouse "after being transported from another state into South Carolina. [FBI agent A.C.] Schlenker said the machines were seized under Public Law 906, passed January 2, 1951, prohibiting the interstate transportation of gambling devices," the Conway *Field* reported.

A decade later, in 1961, a new federal antiracketeering law was passed, and the FBI went on the hunt for illegal gambling.

The Myrtle Beach Elks Club was raided in June 1962, and Horry County police officers "seized nine slot machines, two cases of unopened (quarts) whiskey and 26 opened quarts," according to a report in the *Sun News*.

In October 1963, two Myrtle Beach men, Ira "Cooter" Jennings and Joe Lamar Boring, were charged with "conspiracy to violate Federal gambling laws" following a nine-month FBI investigation.

"Jennings owned and operated the Oasis Club on U.S. 501 and at the time of the alleged violations operated the Brookgreen Room in the Ocean Forest Hotel," an account in the *Sun News* says. "The indictment alleges that the defendants kept and operated dice games, black jack tables, dice tables, Nevada Bank boards and other equipment."

Six weeks later, Jennings, Boring and three others pleaded guilty to "conspiracy to causing the mails to be used in collecting gambling debts." Jennings had to pay a $7,500 fine and received a suspended two-year prison sentence with two years' probation. The other men had lesser fines and two years' probation. The sentencing judge was quoted in the *Sun News* as saying, "Gambling has gone on at Myrtle Beach all my life in South Carolina, and until state and local authorities want to stop it, it's not going to stop."

Video poker machines debuted in Las Vegas in 1975, and they were legal in South Carolina starting the same year through a loophole. The loophole was that the machines themselves did not give cash payouts; the players were given credits for "free play," which they then cashed out with a business employee. For the next twenty-five years, as video poker machines' technology became more sophisticated, so did their popularity. You could find them in almost every convenience store, bar and mom-and-pop restaurant. They provided a tidy side income for many small businesses. Lawmakers let South Carolina voters decide in 2000 if they wanted to continue to allow video poker machines to be legal, and the voters said no.

In 2012, a loophole was similarly exploited when strip malls were overrun with "sweepstakes" rooms. Customers "rented" computer time to play video games, and they tried to build up credits that they then redeemed from a sweepstakes room employee. It didn't take long for legislators to plug the loophole, and in 2013, the sweepstakes rooms went out of business.

Video poker and other video gambling machines can still be found in some businesses' backrooms, and sometimes agents from the South Carolina Law Enforcement Division (SLED) seize them. In April 2011, a Murrells Inlet restaurant and bar had a fire early on a Sunday morning, and after firefighters extinguished it, there remained in an upstairs room evenly spaced rows of charred video poker machines. The restaurant owner said he subleased the room to someone else, and he thought the video poker machines were simply being stored there.

From 1974 through 1985, high-stakes sports gambling hit a peak in the Myrtle Beach area. Bookies such as Tyson Leonard were reaping huge amounts of money. His cards and sports betting is legendary, and multiple accounts credit him with being a "high roller" who thought nothing of personally betting tens of thousands of dollars on one golf game.

Tawny Monroe's husband worked for Tyson Leonard. Leonard also had businesses that manufactured aluminum buildings and truck camper shells and was a partner in the Tramps nightclub.

"[Leonard] was a big bookie," Monroe said. "Tons of locally well-known people were booking. My husband was a nightclub manager and a bookie. I remember going through the Miami airport—we were going to Boca Raton to meet Tyson Leonard. [My husband] had thousands of dollars, like $140,000 of booking money…There was big gambling down here. When there was a big game on [television], my husband and his partner… would have their phones and be taking the bets in a golf course condo. Bay Tree golf course was a big booking hub. Tyson handled enforcement, and so, many times, there were close calls thinking the police were coming. Eventually, they did get busted. Tyson was big—he was in charge. It was his operation."

Leonard brought stunt motorcyclist Evel Knievel to Myrtle Beach, and Monroe remembers the daredevil flirted with her and "had a huge ego and was a big bragger." Knievel was also a gambler, and it was at Bay Tree that Knievel said he won $100,000 from Leonard in a golf game.

Some of the high rollers were local tobacco farmers, as journalist Al Blondin reported in 2006 in an award-winning feature article about Tyson Leonard and other gamblers of the period. Eventually, Leonard was arrested with two associates, who were charged, tried and convicted in 1985 for gambling activities. He served a few months of time and was banned from the Grand Strand for five years.

Chapter 8

VENGEANCE

Horry County has had its share of enraged people going to extremes.

ATTORNEY ATTACK

In the spring of 1952, fifty-one-year-old Albert Raymond Reinhart lived with his mother and owned two Myrtle Beach hotels: the Miramar-Reinhart and the Miramar-Terrace. He was active in the community, including helping to organize the Myrtle Beach Hotel Association and was a director of the South Carolina Hotel Association.

Reinhart had previously lived in Wrightsville Beach, North Carolina, where in 1926, his father killed Reinhart's wife by shooting her. A police officer then shot Reinhart's father. As the father lay dying, Reinhart entered his hospital room and hit him with a blackjack. In that case, Reinhart was charged with assault with a deadly weapon.

That information was included in an April 1952 article in the *Field* that told the story of how Reinhart was angry at a North Carolina attorney and former state senator named Emmett H. Bellamy "over the handling of some property of his [Reinhart's] mother." Reinhart decided Bellamy needed to be killed, so he went to a building in Charlotte where he knew the attorney would be, and he waited calmly for more than an hour.

As Bellamy and his law partner, Lloyd Elkins Jr., entered an elevator, Reinhart shot three times. Two bullets struck Bellamy and killed him, and one bullet injured Elkins.

The article said Reinhart showed no remorse at his preliminary hearing, and it quoted him as saying, "I'm not sorry, I'm glad. I came here to kill him and I did."

SHE WOULDN'T SAY YES

In 1905, Belle Sessions, "a young girl of 18 or 20 years of age," according to an article in the *Manning Times*, lived with her mother, Betsy Sessions, and Belle's two young children in the Homewood area north of Conway in "a peaceful looking one-roomed board cabin, surrounded by a small clearing, planted in English peas and

Albert Raymond Reinhart owned the Miramar-Reinhart and the Miramar-Terrace hotels in Myrtle Beach when he shot and killed attorney Emmett H. Bellamy in 1952. *Author's collection.*

HOTELS AND GUEST HOUSES

MIRAMAR TERRACE HOTEL
"OVERLOOKING THE OCEAN"

Air-cooled in summer. Insulated. Private baths. Offering everything to make you comfortable and your stay delightful.

Accommodations Recommended

Two of Myrtle Beach's select places for vacationing. Ocean Boulevard North at 24th Ave. Open year 'round.

European Plan   Rates on Request

Phone 2661

THE MIRAMAR — REINHART
" BY - THE - SEA "

Unexcelled accommodations. Homelike atmosphere. All rooms are large and comfortable with Simmons Beautyrest beds. First-floor bedrooms available. Private or connecting baths. Two spacious living rooms, cool and restful porches, beach house, and hot and cold showers for bathers.

A bountiful and delicious breakfast served from 8 to 10:30 A. M.

Located in preferred resort section.

19

strawberries, in the midst of the pine woods." Neither Belle nor her mother had ever been married.

But a local man, F.O. "Buddie" Sessions (the article does not say if they were related), wanted to marry her. However, Belle did not want to marry Buddie, especially after he made her promise to marry him at gunpoint.

Belle made plans to move to another state to be with another male friend and to get away from Buddie. She purchased train tickets for all four members of her little family, and they were supposed to leave on March 29. However, for some reason, they were still in their cabin on March 30.

Belle's mother left the cabin to do some work, and Buddie, who had been hiding nearby in the woods, went in and pulled Belle outside. Holding her tight with his left hand, he "pulled his revolver of 38 calibre and emptied every chamber into her body at arm's length. After releasing her, she staggered a few steps and fell in the yard, where she was found, with her two small children crying over her." Buddie then reloaded all the gun's chambers and shot himself in the right temple. A note found in his pocket gave directions for paying debts he owed.

Testimony about the matter was given later that day in the cabin's yard, with the jury sitting on top of the woodpile. Buddie Sessions's body lay nearby, and Belle Sessions was outside, mortally wounded, on a quilt.

Timber Dispute

Reverend Harmon Grainger, a Baptist preacher, had been having a dispute with a man named Commander Johnson and his girlfriend, Charlotte Simmons. Grainger said he would not pay for a timber transaction, and he threatened to have the couple arrested for adultery.

The reverend was plowing his cotton field at 9:00 a.m. on June 23, 1905, when Johnson and Simmons crept up on him, and Grainger was shot twice in the back. The couple was arrested right away, and while both were convicted, only Johnson was given the death sentence.

Although it seemed to be an open-and-shut case, Johnson's relatives made so many threats about the upcoming hanging that the local military company, called the Conway Hussars, were sent to guard the jail. On October 20, 1905, Commander Johnson was "the last white man to be hanged in Conway."

Double Duty

If you've ever wondered why Horry County is the only county in South Carolina to have both a county sheriff department and a county police department, the reason goes back to the late 1950s. The sheriff's department was accused of much wrongdoing, including unfair enforcement of laws, accepting bribes, pressuring businesses to patronize certain vendors and abusing prisoners. Charges were brought, but no convictions were made.

In 1959, Horry County delegates in the state legislature decided if they couldn't get rid of the sheriff, they'd circumvent him. They "established the Horry County Police Department, cut the sheriff down to two deputies and abolished the constables. The police department was given a chief and eight policemen. In effect, they replaced the eight constables and 11 deputies," a 1959 article in the *Florence Morning News* says. They moved the sheriff and his two deputies out of their jail office to a smaller space in the courthouse and took away their department's control of the jail.

Operating costs for the sheriff's department from July 1, 1956, through March 31, 1958—a span of twenty-one months—were $132,353.97. Collected fines were $52,239.00, reflecting a net operating cost for almost two years of $75,114.97. During the first year the Horry County Police took over, costs were $67,102.64 and collected fines were $60,524.23, for a net operating cost of almost $7,000.00.

Laughed at the Wrong Guy

In the summer of 1928, the road between Conway and Myrtle Beach was notoriously bad in some places, and car tires were narrow and not suited for navigating washouts. Dr. W.W. Weston of Columbia was piqued when his auto became stuck in a hole. A group of highway department employees were sitting nearby at the side of the road, so the doctor asked them for help. He became outraged when they "threw back their heads and laughed as if it were the funniest thing in the world."

Wrong answer. Dr. Weston had friends in high places, and the next day, he went before a meeting of the South Carolina Highway Commission and told them what happened. The employees' behavior was pronounced "unspeakable" by the chief highway engineer, and "the commission voted to investigate the entire situation at once."

Chapter 9

THIEVES AND THEIR LOOT

Y ou can hear plenty of pirate stories in other books that are more myth than fact, but there are some instances based in reality. There is solid evidence that pirates trolled our coasts and stashed loot here.

One such tale comes from 1951 when a Spanish coin of the type that would have been a favorite of pirates was found at Tilghman Beach, which is now part of North Myrtle Beach. An article in the *Tabor City Tribune* said:

Tilghman Beach was excited this week by the discovery of an ancient coin of unknown origin and age, by C.H. Lewis, caretaker for Tilghman Estates.

Mr. Lewis's find and the discovery of some old iron scrap presumed to come from a ship, revived interest in the rumors that the notorious pirate, Blackbeard, once hid his loot along this coast.

Those who have seen the coin have expressed the opinion it is a Spanish coin, possibly minted in the days when clergy were both temporal and spiritual rulers. This belief is supported by the fact that a large coat of arms topped with a clerical hat or crown is centered on one side. On the opposite side are four shapes of four leaf clover, with smaller insignia, roughly in the circle of wording and abbreviations around the circumference of the coin.

The finder, as well as developers of Tilghman Beach have kept the site of the discovery a secret and efforts are now being made to identify the time and place of minting. A search for additional "loot" is also underway.

EASY PREY

The Civil War (1861–65) might have ended slavery, but it created desperation among southerners, causing some Confederate army deserters to prey on local residents. Women, children and elderly men felt extremely isolated while fending off predatory thieves.

Ellen Cooper Johnson's memoirs about that period include accounts of two deserters' raids in 1865 at Cool Springs, a town a little northwest of Conway. Her tale is a fascinating glimpse into a period when people already exhausted from war faced theft and vandalism from unscrupulous neighbors. It also provides a look at their farm layout, supplies and livelihood.

The deserters' standard operating procedure was to stake out isolated farms where there were only women, children, the elderly and perhaps a few slaves on the property. Part of their reconnaissance was to have someone simply walk by to see what sorts of activities were taking place. Once vulnerabilities and strengths were assessed, they plotted to rob the farm of valuables with the least amount of effort. Walter Hill, director of the Horry County Museum, said that often meant setting a barn on fire to create a diversion. While the family rushed to the fire to save the milk cow, the deserters broke down the smokehouse door and made away with food.

In the case of Ellen Cooper Johnson's family, she wrote:

> *The raiders were deserters from our own army who would lie in the woods and would rather steal from the defenseless families than work or fight for their state…About this time, our two yard dogs had been shot by the deserters. The barn had been broken open, and also the old store where our cotton was stored. They had taken quite a lot of corn and cotton. They worked silently, and we did not know until the next day what had gone on. It seemed they generally made their raids on Saturday nights, knowing that the hands on the place were always away then.*

In the week after that raid, Johnson's family and their "colored servants" busied themselves shucking and shelling their corn and hiding it in the smokehouse, which was close to the main house, and processing several barrels of pork. Johnson's father visited from Conway with other Confederate soldiers who were home on furlough to see if they could find the deserters' camp, but they had no luck.

Saturday: This has been a terrible week with us. We slept little for fear of being killed or burned out. There was nothing to do but to wait and watch, for we were expecting the deserters every minute. It was a beautiful calm moonlit night, but how helpless and lonely we felt! The two old faithful servants had gone to visit their families who lived some distance from Cool Springs. About eight o'clock we saw that a fire had been started on the turpentine still-yard. What could we do? Over one thousand barrels of turpentine and resin were on this yard, and it was burning! My sister told me and the colored girl to run and call old man Bart and his daughter, or they would be burned to death. We ran shouting, "Fire, fire!" but no answer. When we got to the yard, we saw them in the shed which stood a few feet from the road. Old man Bart was throwing out new spirit barrels which had been packed there the first year of the war. He told us to roll these barrels some distance down the road where he thought they would be saved, for [if] the wind rose everything at Cool Springs would be destroyed. We knew that this fire had been set to draw us away from the house. My sister, with the children and the cook had remained there. We finally rolled the last barrel from the shop—what more could be done?

Old man Bart told us that if we could keep the covers of the still and grits mill [sic] wet, we might save them, as they were some distance from the fire. By this time, the fire was spreading, getting higher and higher every minute. There was plenty of water, for the side of this still was a large tank. In this tank was coiled a large pipe, called the "still-worm" which carried the water into the still. This tank was kept full of water at all times to cover the pipe. I knew that steps went to the top of the tank and the upper floor of the still. If I could reach the top of these steps, my shoulders and arms would be above the edge of the roof. I could stand there and throw water with one hand while holding to a scantling which was nailed to the post, with my other hand. I got up, and with a large tin dipper, I dipped water from the tank and threw it as far as I could up on the smoldering roof. I was wet from head to foot. While I was up there, Miss Celie (old man Bart's daughter) was on top of the mill shed throwing water. The flames were now higher than the tallest pine tree and seemed to go straight upwards—not a breeze was stirring, for it was a calm, beautiful night— thick black clouds of smoke floated high above us.

Fortunately the melting resin ran down the side of the hill, carrying the flames farther from us. The heat was unbearable, but the night was cool, and our clothing was wet. What an awful night! My arms ached. I would stop and rest, then go back to work again. While Miss Celie and I were at our posts, Old Man Bart was picking up the burning pieces of resin which were falling all around us and starting new fires. We commenced our work about midnight, and we stayed there and worked until day. We then went back to the house and found that my sister and the cook had been up all night watching for the deserters. The fire was still burning—it burned for days afterwards—but the house was not in danger.

Sunday: What a lonely day, and how helpless we felt! I was very hoarse and could not speak above a whisper. My hands and arms were swollen, and pained so that I could not use them for several days. My head ached. I was sick. I could not give up. Sister had all that she could bear, and I must help her all that I could. The danger of the fire was over—but what next?

What came next was word sent from Georgetown that Yankees were on the way. Johnson wrote that she didn't know what was worse, the Yankees or the deserters. To protect themselves, they packed a large box with "the best things that were in the house," including dishes, glassware, clothing and linens. They buried the box in a hole under the floor of their smokehouse. They also buried one barrel each of syrup, pork and corn in their mules' stalls.

The next raid was a week after the first.

On Friday night there was another raid! We did not know of it until the next morning. The first thing I saw was a large pile of dirt thrown up on each side of the smokehouse door. I was afraid to go to the smokehouse for fear that the raiders were inside. I called for my sister, Lou, to come, so that we could go in together and see what had been done. There was no one there. A large hole had been dug under the door. It was four or five feet deep and as wide. We saw many tracks around where they had dragged the box out. Our box was gone! Sister said "What shall we do!" I could not reply. I was speechless. We looked around and found that they had torn down the yard fence and had driven a cart into the yard. They had not broken open the smoke-house for fear of making a noise. By digging under the door, they did not enter above the dirt floor. None of the provisions had been taken—but, oh our box! We thought that we had hidden it so carefully. Of course we must have been watched by someone.

Another raid came two days later, and a male neighbor (who later became Johnson's husband) was at their home with his rifle while Johnson and her sister had pistols. The raiders came in the middle of the night again, and there was an exchange of gunfire. Bullets crashed into the house, including into a wardrobe they pulled in front of a bed to protect the children.

No one was shot, but the next morning revealed the raiders had destroyed the smokehouse and took barrels of corn and pork stored there as well as fifty-eight hams and all the salt they had—a few bushels. The raiders left behind "one lone ham and some of the shoulder meat."

Johnson sent word to her father, who was in Conwayborough, and the area's Home Guard responded. They searched nearby woods, and eventually one of the deserters was captured.

> He was a young man…He was tied to a tree in the yard and was told that the law for deserters from the army was death. He begged them to spare his life, and if they would, he would tell them the names of all the men who were in the raid, and where to find the things that had been taken away. The corn and pork barrels were hidden in the swamp; the things in the box had been divided up, and were in the houses of different raiders. Sister Lou and I sat on the porch and heard this conversation. He was taken to jail and tried. He gave the names of those who were in the raid. Some of them had been wounded, and all of them had escaped except this one. Capt. Ervin, with his [Home Guard] company, was busy hunting the raiders for a week or more. They took mules and wagons and brought in most of the provisions which had been hidden in the swamp—and also some of the things which had been in our box. These were found in the homes of the raiders as the boy had said. This corn and pork which we had hidden in the stall was never found.
>
> About this time, Capt. Ervin was called to Conway, as raiding was going on there, too. Warehouses were opened, cotton as well as provisions were taken. Not satisfied with this, they went down the river and made raids on the rice mills. Returning, one of them was shot and killed on the farther side of the river near the foot of the present bridge—and another, further down the road. Still another was killed at Board Landing. After this, the raiding stopped. These raiders were deserters from our own army, which was a terrible thing.

LOWER THAN HORSE THIEVES

Walter Hill, director of the Horry County Museum in Conway, said it wasn't uncommon for someone to own a 250-plus-acre farm and cultivate only 20

Families and close friends helped one another cut wood, and they hoped no one stole their piles. *William Van Auken Greene collection, Horry County Museum, Conway, South Carolina.*

acres. The rest might be used for timbering, turpentine production or as their own personal woodlot. If a family had plenty of trees on their property, they could become part of a series of cool-weather wood cutting parties.

First, the family had to figure out how much wood they needed during the year for heating, cooking, soap making, clothes washing, bathing, hog scalding, tobacco curing and more. It amounted to several cords, and green wood had to be cut and stacked in advance so it would cure and dry enough to burn steadily and put out heat.

Once the year's fall harvests were finished and pesky bugs were killed off with first frosts, the wood cutting parties started.

"They're going to turn around and on a weekend, maybe on a Saturday, everybody might come to my place and we'd all go out and have a wood cutting party," Hill said. "[We'd be] cutting and stacking it…Sawing, dragging trees, cutting them into stove-wood length, or other needed sizes. Often stacking it right there in the woods and going back later to get it. You're going to let it season right there in the woods."

Since an inexpensive supply of cured firewood was critical for small tobacco farmers' success—you couldn't cure barns full of tobacco without a lot of aged wood—stealing from a family's forest woodlot was a crime on the level of horse thievery.

"It took what was considered the lowest among thieves to mess with a man's wood lot," Walter Hill said. "When it came time to cure your tobacco, when it starts, it starts. There's no stopping in the middle of it…So it would take the sorriest of sorry thieves to go to a man's wood lot and take his tobacco curing wood and burn it. On occasion that happened, and those people were ostracized. They're just low down and sorry."

Three Gallons of Milk a Day

In October and November 1950, a rash of livestock thefts had small farmers scrambling to protect their pigs and cows. An article dated November 15, 1950, in the *Tabor City Tribune* is headlined "Cattle Rustling Flourishing Throughout Upper Horry." The way it's written is humorous.

Cattle rustling is still going on in this modern age when most people thought it went out of style when the old west became civilized.

At least three cows have been rustled in upper Horry County within the last five weeks, at least five hogs have gone the same way and to date there is no clue as to how the slick bunch of lawbreakers are doing the job.

Just to make the crime more unusual, most of the thievery is taking place…while people are attending church.

Last Sunday night a red jersey milk cow, owned by Ernest Hayes of Green Sea was stolen from her stable in the barn while Mr. and Mrs. Hayes were at church. She was a black tongued cow, dark from her knees to her hoofs, had curved horns, signs of chain marks around horns, was about seven years old, gave three gallons of milk a day and weighed about 700 pounds.

Two sets of plow lines were missing from the Hayes' barn and it is presumed that the cow was led off with the lines, loaded in a truck and carried away. All efforts to locate her at various stock yards throughout the area have been unsuccessful thus far.

Hayes this week posted a $100.00 reward for information leading to the recovery of the cow. Any persons knowing the whereabouts of this cow can claim the reward by getting her back to Mr. Hayes at Green Sea.

Mose Hodge, also of Green Sea, lost a yearling the same way on Thursday night three weeks ago. She was taken from her barn stable.

Tuney Grainger, who lives in the section near Carolina Baptist Church, had a milk cow stolen five weeks ago on Sunday night; again the theft was made while the owner was at church, Graingers's cow was tied near the house at the time she was rustled.

On Tuesday night November 7, Watson Shelley, in the same Green Sea area, lost five hogs to the gang.

Thus far the only possible clue to the rustlers is a vague hunch that the persons doing the rustling is the same outfit that came through the section a few days ago inquiring as to where they could buy a cow. Driving a truck and in a rather suspicious manner, inquiries were made in the community by white men. However, no one suspected anything at the time and the model of truck, license plate or nothing could be recalled by those persons who had seen them.

In a stunning turn of events, the next week's headline on November 22 was "Rustled Horry Cow Found."

The Red Jersey cow that was rustled from the farm of Ernest Hayes in the Green Sea community two weeks ago has been found in Summerton, S.C.

Immediately after the cow was stolen from her stable on Sunday night while Mr. and Mrs. Hayes were attending church, Hayes placed circulars and advertising throughout the area announcing a $100 reward for her return.

The reward brought results Tuesday when word was received that she was on the farm of a man near Summerton. Hayes investigated the report and found the cow. The farmer had purchased the cow in Manning, S.C., for $109 according to reports. The farmer received the reward.

Sheriff's deputies allegedly have a man under arrest and in the county jail at Sumter, S.C. His identity could not be learned today.

MAIL THIEF?

In the fall of 1950, a former Myrtle Beach school superintendent named Ernest F. Southern was sentenced to a year in jail after he pleaded guilty on the charge of stealing letters from the mail. However, a month later, he was released on a $2,500 bond and granted a new trial after Southern told the judge he "did not fully understand the proceedings of the first trial."

The charges stemmed from Southern "taking mail addressed to his secretary, Miss Caroline D. Johnson." At the first trial, evidence included a sworn statement from Johnson signed "immediately after Southern's arrest" that stated, "I have not authorized Ernest F. Southern to take, open, read or destroy any of my mail." At the clemency hearing a month later,

Miss Johnson's testimony changed when she said that "she had given Mr. Southern keys to her box at one time with instructions to open her mail."

The article did not say what was in her mail.

Mule Thief

In August 1951, according to this article in the *Tabor City Tribune*, you could have seen a mule thief at Ocean Drive Beach, which is now part of North Myrtle Beach.

> *Animal antics reached a new high in ludicrousness Monday when a mule, owned by an amusement concession operator, made a mad run down Ocean Drive Beach's crowded main street with a bathroom sink tied to his bridle.*
>
> *The mule had been tied by his owner to the 60-pound cast iron lavatory behind Griste's Drug Store when a snake frightened it. With the sink bouncing behind him, the mule ran through an alley and through the business district, doing more than $100 worth of damage to three parked automobiles.*
>
> *The animal was finally caught when the lavatory got wedged between two parking posts at the Ocean Drive Pavilion.*

Fast Response

Buck Ward owned a country store about eleven miles north of Conway in August 1962. Tony Samora, age twenty-two, was out on parole even though he was previously "serving a life term for murder," according to the *Sun News*. Samora's friend Otis Hood had recently escaped from a North Carolina prison camp.

Samora and Hood headed for the beach on that painfully hot (ninety-six degrees in Conway) day, and they acquired traveling money along the way. First, they stole a Chevrolet Corvair in Asheboro, North Carolina. In Dillon, they sold the car owner's golf clubs for fifteen dollars and then traded a shotgun for a .22-caliber pistol.

When they spotted Buck Ward's store, they drove by three times to case it. The article quotes Ward as saying, "They could see I didn't have a telephone. That, I figure is why he (Tony Sanora) just had me lie down instead of shooting me or hitting me over the head. They figured I couldn't notify the law as fast as I did."

They figured wrong. Samora came in the store, asked for directions, calmly flashed his gun, told Ward to lie on the floor and took $100 out of the cash register. The thief left behind, Ward said, $100 in coins, $500 in another drawer and $100 in his wallet. As soon as the Corvair "spun from the driveway," Ward said he jumped up and retrieved his own gun, but by the time he got outside with it, the car was too far away to even get its license plate number.

The storeowner ran a quarter mile to a telephone and called the South Carolina Highway Patrol and then the county police.

> *Within minutes the patrol, county police and sheriff's department converged on the area and picked up the two's trail. One patrolman lost the pair on a dirt road. Another met them and gave chase along with a county police patrol car. Minutes later, the two abandoned the car and took to the corn field. Shortly the bloodhound was on the trail and 15 minutes later the two, with hands over their heads, walked into the waiting arms of the officers.*

Within an hour of the robbery, officers had returned to Ward's store with the crooks so he could identify them.

"'Samora told me he was sorry,' Ward said. 'I told him the only thing he was sorry about was missing the $600 and underestimating my ability to notify the police. He had his nerve telling me he was sorry.'"

INCORRIGIBLE

Two Conway boys ages twelve and thirteen had authorities running in circles in October 1962. Their names weren't given in a *Sun News* article about their escapades, but the story starts when they "committed a series of break-in robberies in downtown Conway." They were caught and let out on bond. While out on bond, they stole a car from a lumberyard and were arrested after they abandoned the vehicle.

When in court on the charge of car theft, the judge decided to send them to a "semi-private home for boys in North Carolina." While that was being arranged, the boys were put on probation. While on probation, they broke into Conway Elementary School and stole several items, and then on the same night, they went to the Conway Masonic Lodge and stole a car. A police officer caught them near Nixon's Crossroad.

That night, they escaped from the jail and went to the North Myrtle Beach area. From there, the boys said, they got a ride with a Myrtle Beach taxi driver and spent Sunday on the beach. On Monday, they hitched a ride back to Conway, broke into a poolroom and stole twelve dollars, and then, they went home.

Their parents called the police, who took them back to jail and made sure the boys were in a cell from which they couldn't escape.

EASY PICKINGS

In the days before electronic security systems routinely guarded empty buildings, vacant Myrtle Beach vacation homes were easy pickings for determined burglars. In the spring of 1963, the *Sun News* reported, a house owned by a resident of New Bern, North Carolina, was cleaned out. No one even knew the house was robbed until police were tipped off by a phone call.

When Myrtle Beach Police officers went to check it out, they discovered it was empty. Everything was stolen, including "the television set, lamps, pictures from the walls…staples from the kitchen and the meat from the deep freeze." They even carried off a "half-used box of corn flakes."

Police determined the burglar(s) entered through a locked window and carried the home's contents out the front door. The thieves relocked the window and door before leaving.

SUIT STASH

During the summer of 1965, beachgoers in the Ocean Drive area of North Myrtle Beach reported their bathing suits being stolen. An article in the Conway *Field & Herald* does not say exactly from where the suits were snatched, but likely they had been hung outside to dry.

It took a few months, but with the help of "recruit trainees and junior police," some fifty bathing suits were recovered in early January 1966.

"Chief of Police Merlin Bellamy was out with the group of boys who assist the Ocean Drive Police training two young bloodhounds recently given to the department when a cache located 500 yards from a firebreak was spotted by the hounds. A pasteboard box covered with a door was found which contained approximately 50 swim suits."

This discovery led to the arrest of a young man who worked at the beach that summer. The bathing suits were cleaned, and the police department sent letters to people who reported their bathing suits stolen in hopes of returning them to their owners.

Chapter 10
SLIGHTLY WICKED OR PERHAPS JUST FUNNY

For all their gruffness and sternness about being independent, Grand Stranders love a good laugh. But sometimes, the line between being wicked and being funny gets blurred.

For example, it's hard to not chuckle at the mental image created by this story from around 1910 or '12 that Lillian Mills's* father shared with her. Her father was about thirteen or fifteen years old at the time, she said, and he lived with his family in what is now known as the Forestbrook area of Myrtle Beach, back then called the Folly.

> *There was a black man who was married to an Indian lady. Everybody in the area thought that he was a conjure doctor…Everybody was kind of in awe of Indians in this area. They had all gone by that time…His name was Barney Jack, and he became friends with my dad, because my Dad loved to hunt and he did, too…To enhance what people already believed, he got my dad in with him, and they would go to people's wells, and they would put their shoes on backwards and walk around the well. They thought [my dad and Barney Jack] were putting a hex on them or poisoning the water maybe. Sometimes they would even dig a new well. You have to realize it was very, very rural here, and everybody did kind of believe in black magic…There is a man who lived on this street. When he died he believed my daddy had put a hex on him. He really did.*
>
> *So that was one of the things that I guess was evil in a way. Ornery as heck, wasn't it? They didn't have anything to do on Sundays and Saturdays*

except to go fishing and [things] *like that, and he said they would go like they were coming to the beach fishing. They had to walk everywhere. On the way back home, they would hide behind the tombstones down on First Avenue…the Withers Swash Cemetery. They would hide behind the tombstones when they started back home, my dad and his friends, and then the other men who had gone fishing—I'm speaking of cast netting at night—they would start home, and* [my dad and his friends] *would jump out and scare the living bejesus out of them.* [The fishermen] *dropped their fish, so they would get the fish a lot of times.*

FLEEING THE TAX MAN

In 1949, J.R. Lawrimore, a "deputy tax collector," had a warrant to arrest John K. Owens for failure to pay poll taxes amounting to about thirty-five dollars. Poll taxes were one way of preventing people with low incomes, including African Americans, from voting. The tax collector found Owens walking along the street and arrested him. An article about it continues:

Owens then begged the collector to go with him to the office of J.M. Lee, the head tax collector at the courthouse to see if he could find anything wrong with the charges and probably get the head collector to fix bond before the magistrate so that Owens would not have to go to jail on Monday night.

After making the arrest the two walked along from down town to the courthouse. The deputy opened the front door and let Owens inside the courthouse. The deputy then went to the drinking fountain in the hallway and got a drink of water, in the meantime thinking the colored man was right behind him. But the colored man was not behind him. He had slipped backward and outward. The deputy got back to the front door in time to see the end of Owens' coattail as he ran round the corner at the chicken store at the corner of 3rd Avenue and Elm Street. The deputy could not find the negro up town and gave it up for the day.

CHICKEN BOG CAPERS

Picture a group of bored male teenagers who, in the 1920s, are assigned the task of tending the slow-burning fires in tobacco curing barns. To alleviate their boredom, they came up with a creative way to pass the time: chicken bog parties that involved a bit of thievery.

Chicken bog is a traditional Horry County one-pot dish with chicken and rice as its main ingredients.

"In Aynor I attended my first chicken bog—something else I'd never heard of upstate," wrote Mrs. G.W. Collier for the *Independent Republic Quarterly*. "Becoming bored, the young men planned parties. They would secure an iron pot and snitch their neighbors' chickens! Often the owner of the chickens would be a guest, enjoy the bog to the fullest, not knowing that he was eating his own bird! For 'twas always a great secret where the chickens came from. You can imagine the sly looks, quips, nods and becks that ensued. A bog afforded much merriment and finally the host let the fellow know that he had furnished the chickens…Watermelons, also snitched by the young blades, were cut for dessert."

REPRIMAND THREATENED

Anyone who grew up in the 1950s (or has seen the movie *A Christmas Story*) understands that it was common in those days for children to have air rifles. Their use became so popular in the Grand Strand area that one town had to take stern measures.

The Tabor City Town Board voted in February 1952 to "warn all youngsters with air rifles that they must use them on their own premises only and must be used with caution." If they didn't follow those instructions, the town leaders said the offenders would be "brought before the mayor for reprimanding and that parents would have to accompany them. This action was taken because of numerous cases of damage inflicted on animals and property by careless handling of air rifles within the city limits."

PROVOKING INTERSTELLAR WAR

In the early 1950s, there were several incidents of people sighting what they called "flying saucers" throughout Horry County. Mark C. Garner said he even saw one, and he was the well-respected mayor of Myrtle Beach, president of the Myrtle Beach Chamber of Commerce and publisher of the *Sun News*.

One incident in February 1953 prompted local law enforcement officials to urge citizens to not shoot at flying saucers.

Horace Carter reported in the *Tabor City Tribune* about a twenty-nine-year-old military veteran named Lloyd C. Booth who was a farmer from the Poplar-Adrian community in Horry County. Booth was described as having "exceedingly high character." About 11:30 p.m. on January 29, 1953, Booth heard mules neighing in the barn, and then chickens and ducks began squawking. The day before, one of his cows had suddenly died, and the veterinarian said it had been poisoned. He grabbed a pistol and went outside.

Above the pine tops he saw a "strange object."

> *The object was almost still, like it was drifting at a pace lower than the fast walk of a human. It was only some ten feet above the tree tops and easily visible. It was making a very low humming noise, barely detectable. Booth, realizing he was perhaps getting the best view in history of the long discussed "flying saucer," yelled loud and long for someone at the house, about 200 yards away.*

No one in the house awoke, and Booth walked into the woods until he was directly under the saucer.

> *It was about 24 feet long and about 12 feet across, was a light grayish color and was lit up on the inside. Two places in the front resembled strange cockpits and were gassed over. I could see the light inside but could see no object in there. The back also had something resembling a cockpit with a stained glass over it. Light was coming through this section but I could not see through it. The object was about eight or ten feet deep. The front sloped upward at the base at an angle of about 60 degrees and the back was sloped upward at an angle of 40 to 50 degrees. The sides came straight down from the top for maybe four or five feet and then sloped outward and joined the base at about a 45-degree angle.*

The object, Booth told Carter, looked like "half an egg cut from end to end," and he described landing gear. He looked for identifying marks but saw none. "There was no possible means of support for the object," he said. "It had no propeller, there were no exhaust fume[s] showing, no vapor trail and I could detect no unusual odor. It simply sat there and drifted along as I ran around and around it getting just as good a look as I could."

After watching it for twenty to thirty minutes, Booth

fired his pistol straight up at the "saucer" at a distance of about 75 feet. "I heard the bullet hit the object. It made a metallic sound and bounced off. I fired again but did not hear the bullet hit. A bare instant later, the object began making considerably more noise like a large electric motor and took off at a high rate of speed at about a 65 degree angle. It kept that same course until it was completely out of sight."

The article concludes by emphasizing that Booth was "a Christian who doesn't drink" and mentioning that "18 cows died mysteriously in Horry County in the last 18 weeks, from poisoning" as well as a great number of hogs. One farmer lost all seventy-five of his hogs.

Motorcycle Acrobats

Myrtle Beach has been a popular destination for motorcycle enthusiasts since roads connected it with the outside world. In the winter of 1952, a group of bikers who wanted to get a little wild were joined by the Ocean Drive (now a part of North Myrtle Beach) chief of police. A report from Claude Dunnagan in the *Tabor City Tribune* says:

On Sunday, about 30 motorcycles roared into Ocean Drive Beach, and out onto our beautiful, wide, flat smooth strand where they cut loose with some hair-raising 2-wheeled acrobatics. Police Chief Merlin Bellamy suggested they move slightly north beyond Ocean Drive city limits, which they gladly did and proceeded to make a race track of the Grand Strand between Tilghman Beach and Ocean Drive Beach. One rider clocked off 120 miles per hour on his souped-up vehicle. Chief Bellamy, who is a cycling enthusiast himself, rode one over a hundred miles per hour.

Mom Bomb

During August 1953, a mother in Cherry Grove Beach (now part of North Myrtle Beach) was fed up with her two young sons setting off firecrackers, and she forbade them from buying any more. Precisely following her instructions, they went to Frank Boulineau's grocery store and did not buy firecrackers. They bought a "torpedo with a fuse on it" instead.

Their mother saw it when they got back to the house, and, according to a newspaper account, they told her it was a

> *smoke-bomb for getting rid of mosquitoes. The explanation obviously satisfied the mother, and she put the thing up on a kitchen shelf. That night, while cooking supper, she noticed some mosquitoes buzzing around the dining room table. Remembering the mosquito smoke-bomb she'd gotten from her two sons, she placed it on the table and lit the fuse. Then she walked casually back to the stove to salt some garden peas she was cooking. WHAM!*
>
> *Grocer Boulineau, getting the report direct from the distracted mother the following day, tallied the damages as follows: One ruined table cloth, several broken dishes, a bad case of shocked nerves, a whole box of salt dropped into a pot of peas, and two paddled posteriors.*

Chapter 11

KLUXED

For a period of three years in the early 1950s, more than ten years before the first area school was integrated, an uprising in Horry County of the Ku Klux Klan resulted in chaos. There were several floggings of both white and black people, one Klan member died, a thriving and historically important African American music legacy was extinguished and, for the first time, a Pulitzer Prize was awarded to a weekly newspaper. While people who were brutalized by the Klan lived through terror, in hindsight, this particular Klan resurgence bordered on comical. The ringleader was in it for the money, and he exploited residents' fears, prejudices and religion to bilk them for thousands of dollars.

DOMINATION, DESPERATION AND DETERMINATION

American white domination of people with dark-colored skin started in colonial times. Most Native Americans who weren't killed by settlers either died from European diseases or were forced to move from their ancestral lands, and an entire race was almost completely erased from the South Carolina coast within about one hundred years.

In 1770, William Bull II wrote in a letter to the Earl of Hillsboro, "I cannot quit the Indians without mentioning an observation that has often raised my wonder. That in this Province, settled in 1670…Then swarming

Chicora Wood was one of seven Georgetown County rice plantations owned by former South Carolina governor Robert F.W. Allston (1801–1864). He had hundreds of slaves who worked his rice fields. *Photograph by Charles N. Bayless. Library of Congress, Prints and Photographs Division.*

with tribes of Indians, there remain now, except the few Catawbas, nothing of them but their names, within three hundred miles of our seacoast."

By then, about 90 percent of the area's Native Americans were gone or were enslaved. Ironically, around the same time William Bull II wrote

Shown here in 1936 or 1937 in a photograph by Frances Benjamin Johnston, the Georgetown clock tower was once the site of slave auctions. *Library of Congress, Prints and Photographs Division, Carnegie Survey of the Architecture of the South.*

his letter, the area's population was 90 percent black slaves. Most of the slaves in the Grand Strand area lived on rice plantations around Georgetown, but Horry County also had its share. In 1850, Horry County had a population of 7,646, according to an article by John Thomas in the fall 1982 issue of the *Independent Republic Quarterly*. He listed 5,522 whites and 2,075 slaves. In Georgetown County, there were 2,193 white residents and 18,253 slaves.

It was common for slaves to be willed to family members. In 1819, the price of a healthy eighteen-year-old male was $700, which equates to about $13,000 in 2015. Listings in an Horry County deed book dated 1811–37 includes:

> *Samuel Garrell to William McQueen, Junr. $200. Negro girl Esther Johann. 15 Oct 1812. S/ Samuel Garrell. W/ Daniel McQueen, Daniel Johnston. Aff: Daniel Johnston 15 Oct 1812. Recd 2 Nov 1819.*

This slave cabin is at Chicora Wood Plantation in Georgetown County. Chicora Wood's owner, Robert F.W. Allston, had 630 slaves in 1860 according to the National Park Service. *Photograph by Charles N. Bayless, Library of Congress, Prints and Photographs Division.*

*93 Willis Rawls to John Hall. $300. Negro boy Tom. 3 Nov 1812. S/
W. Rawls. W/ John Harlee, William McQueen. Aff: William McQueen
5 Nov 1819. Recd 5 Nov 1819.*

*94 James Graham to wife, Elizabeth. Gw/a. All land & household
goods, certain slaves. To dau. Jane, slaves; to dau. Maretia, slaves; dau.
Elizabeth, slaves; son John, slaves; son William, slaves, dau. Sarah Ann,
slaves. 6 May 1817. S/ James Graham. W/ William H. Grice, John
Gunter. Aff. Wm. H. Grice. 22 Oct 1817. Recd 5 Nov 1819.*

*Willis Rawls to Thomas Garrell. $700. Negro boy Elick, age 18. 16
Sep 1819. S/ W. Rawls, Marguritte (x) Rawls. W/ Samuell Floyd
Min_r_., Arthur H. Crawford. Aff. Samuell Floyd 24 Sep 1819.*

Struggle for Equality

Following emancipation, African Americans and Native Americans
continued to be victims of white dominance. Sometimes that dominance was
violent, but mostly it manifested in day-to-day life when people of color were
not allowed to sit with whites on public transportation, in movie theaters or
restaurants; drink from the same water fountains; or attend the same schools.
Horry County had a "'deadline' that ran from the north-central town of
Loris to the western town of Aynor. Any African-American who did not
already live west of the line was not allowed to cross it," according to a 2009
Horry County historic property survey.

However, the line relaxed over the years, and many "black sections" existed
in most communities, even east of the deadline. Before the civil rights era that
started in the early 1950s, those sections are where blacks had to live unless they
wanted to incur wrath from whites. Only whites served on juries back then, so it
was rare for whites to be convicted of crimes against African Americans.

Rise of the Klan

Many people don't realize there are several documented cases in Horry
County of the Ku Klux Klan inflicting vigilante justice on white people

who were deemed drunks, wife-beaters or otherwise worthy of a beating. This Klan targeted people who weren't Christian, sober, gainfully employed or married (if living with someone of the opposite sex) in addition to intimidating people of color.

The Ku Klux Klan originally got its start after the Civil War in Georgia, and its leader, or Imperial Wizard, was Nathan Bedford Forrest. His group of robed and masked vigilantes dedicated themselves to ensuring that blacks worked in fields and Republicans were not in power. David M. Chalmers wrote in *Hooded Americanism: The History of the Ku Klux Klan* that "the death toll of Negroes and Republicans probably ran close to a thousand."

South Carolinians weren't particularly active in this early KKK. "In South Carolina, the Klan could seldom even count on countywide co-operation among its members," and its densest concentrations were in the middle to western parts of the state. That first KKK was short-lived, and by 1871, it no longer existed.

Resurgences

The Ku Klux Klan significantly resurged twice: during World War I and in the 1940s and '50s following World War II. The World War I resurgence started in 1915 in Georgia, but it quickly overtook the entire nation, stretching through the Midwest and as far as California. In the 1920s, Klansmen were elected to local and even national offices with a message of "the protection of traditional American values," Chalmers wrote. The Klan's American membership swelled to as many as five million at its peak in the mid-1920s, and its organizers made a lot of money. The initiation fee was $10.00, which was divvied up by five higher-ups in the chapter. New members also paid $6.50 for their masks and robes, and if they rode a horse, there was an additional fee of $14.00 for the horse's robe. The Gate City Manufacturing Company of Atlanta had a monopoly on hood and robe sales. Another revenue stream was selling "special Ku Klux water" for $10.00 per quart that was used in initiation exercises.

The Klan had a parade in Conway on September 18, 1923, around the same time the racist movie *Birth of a Nation*, which depicted Klan members as saviors of southern gentility, made its Conway debut. About twenty cars rolled through Conway about 9:00 p.m. that Tuesday night. The lead car had a "firey cross" on the front, and the cars were "full of white robed figures."

COPYRIGHT—1923.
THE HAMMOND STUDIOS,
MERIDIAN, AND JACKSON, MISS

About the time this photograph of Klan initiation rites was taken in 1923 in Mississippi, the first Horry County KKK parade was held in Conway. *Library of Congress, Prints and Photographs Division.*

On September 20, 1923, the *Horry Herald* reported, "Horry County has had a flogging, equal to any of those of which you have read in print in dispatches from other states."

The incident happened on a Friday night when about fifty to seventy-five men "in hooded masks" went to the farm of John Rogers "near Finklea's Cross Roads, six miles west of Loris" and kidnapped a woman who was a tenant farmer there. They then kidnapped Rogers, a married man who was working that night as a deputy sheriff on the hunt for whiskey stills, from the car he was riding in with a police officer. The hooded men took Rogers and the woman to a spot "on the Zoan road not far above the Placard bridge" and cut their hair off.

In 1925, a Klan parade with more than 40,000 participants marched down Pennsylvania Avenue in Washington, D.C. By the time the Great Depression overtook America in the early 1930s, its ranks had dwindled from 5 million to about 100,000. The reasons for its waning were due to distaste for many members' extremism, a realization that its principles were

immoral and irreligious and a well-publicized case in Indiana when a Klan leader kidnapped and raped a twenty-eight-year-old schoolteacher, who subsequently died due to effects of the attack.

The Ku Klux Klan never completely died out during the Great Depression, and its remaining members' activities became more secretive. Night riding (terrorism dealt out under the cover of darkness) remained a main threat. It gained some members who were opposed to the rise of labor unions that sought equality for workers regardless of race, but the KKK was dealt a crippling financial blow in 1944. The U.S. Bureau of Internal Revenue "filed a lien for back taxes of over $685,000 on profits earned during the 1920s," Chalmers wrote. The Klan had to sell most of its assets in order to pay the bill.

After World War II is when Horry County saw the most visible and vocal examples of the Ku Klux Klan. But this was not the same Klan of the antebellum or post–World War I Invisible Empire. This was a new renegade Klan called the Association of Carolina Klans, one of several splinter factions of the Associated Klans of America.

With many young men home from World War II, the relative boredom of rural life made KKK membership sound intriguing to some of them. It

The Ku Klux Klan marched on Pennsylvania Avenue in Washington, D.C., on September 13, 1926. *Library of Congress, Prints and Photographs Division, Photograph by National Photo Co.*

didn't help that South Carolina politics were spawning an extremely racist period. In 1948, a national political party called the Dixiecrats was founded with South Carolina governor J. Strom Thurmond (1902–2003) as its presidential nominee. Its party platform called for "segregation of the races and the racial integrity of each race." A common reason given by whites to keep segregation in effect was to "protect" both races. "Our segregation laws in the South were not enacted for the purpose of discriminating against, or to humiliate the Negro," says a 1949 article in the *Horry Herald*, "but were enacted to protect both races from trouble."

GRAND THEFT DRAGON

It was in this environment of turmoil and prejudice that an enterprising former grocer named Thomas L. Hamilton (1907–1976) moved to the South Carolina town of Leesville, in the Midlands. Proclaiming himself the South Carolina KKK Grand Dragon, Hamilton set up a cottage industry through KKK membership fees, robe and hood sales, the sale of racist literature and more.

Hamilton also orchestrated wreaking havoc in Horry County. In the summer of 1950, as the civil rights movement gained momentum, Hamilton stirred up racial resentments and drummed up KKK memberships with many nighttime parades and cross burnings throughout coastal South Carolina. The parades were terrifying motorcades with long lines of cars cruising through town. The lead car had a cross on front that was rigged with menacing red lights. The cars' occupants were dressed in Klan robes and hoods, and they had the dome lights on so people on the streets could see them. Sometimes they displayed guns.

Tabor City is a small town in North Carolina alongside the South Carolina and Horry County lines. Its nickname is Razor City because of its reputation for vicious fights. When the law came after them, the brawlers would scatter and try to get across the state line because officers usually didn't pursue into the neighboring state.

Beginning in 1950, the editor of the *Tabor City Tribune*, Horace Carter (1921–2009), doggedly documented Klan activities throughout Horry County. The July 12, 1950 issue has an article headlined "KK Klan Puts on Parade in Conway; Horry County Said to Have 3,500 Members." It reads:

> *On a recent Saturday night the Ku Klux Klan went on parade in Conway, with 40 cars carrying the robed figures through the principal streets of Horry's county seat.*
>
> *There were no estimates of the number of robed individuals in the parade, but all cars carried several Klansmen. After its ghostly tour through the main streets, the cavalcade wound through the colored section.*

Horace Carter, editor of the *Tabor City Tribune*, earned his newspaper a Pulitzer Prize for his coverage of Ku Klux Klan activities in Horry County and surrounding areas. *Photograph courtesy* Tabor City Tribune.

Reports are that the cavalcade gathered near the Yauhannah Bridge and that robes, hoods and insignia of the order were donned there. It is also said that the lead car carried a fiery-like cross, marking the leader of the band.

"A DIABOLICAL AND OUTRAGEOUS AFFAIR"

Lillian Mills* remembers one of those Klan motorcades taking place in Myrtle Beach the evening of August 26, 1950. It was one of the more infamous parades.

Twenty-seven Klan cars cruised slowly through Myrtle Beach that Saturday night, and their itinerary included driving by Charlie's Place at Whispering Pines, a black-owned nightclub where some of the nation's most well-known black entertainers, such as Little Richard and Aretha Franklin, performed. Klan members had previously threatened the club's owner, Charlie Fitzgerald, over allowing admittance to young whites who were lured by the music and dancing.

"Integration was at night. Segregation was during the day," Roddy Brown said in November 2014. He was a child in the 1950s, and he remembers many young white locals and tourists visiting Charlie's Place. They slipped in late at night to listen to music by black artists and to dance an early form of the shag, but many people didn't like whites and blacks dancing together or such progressive attitudes.

Charlie Fitzgerald was known as a sharp dresser. He usually wore suspenders as well as a pistol or two in shoulder holsters. Local restaurateur Dino Thompson remembers being amazed once when, to do some work, Fitzgerald wore overalls—they were starched. Fitzgerald had friendly relationships with local white law enforcement officers, and he didn't put up with fights or similar mayhem at his establishment.

Mills saw the motorcade go by her house as it left Myrtle Beach and headed north to Atlantic Beach to intimidate its black residents. She said it was puzzling that the cars came by her house, located on a dirt side street, when they could have taken U.S. 17, which was paved. She guessed that their

This 1949 photograph taken in Florida has an electrified cross like many people in Horry County remember from Ku Klux Klan motorcades in the early 1950s, including the one that led to the shootout at Charlie's Place in Myrtle Beach. *AP photograph.*

route had to do with menacing either a notorious drunk who lived on the street or any Jews who happened to be at the nearby temple.

"The children and I were here," Mills said. "I can remember that I was holding [my baby] on my hip…We heard these sirens coming down our street, which you hardly never heard. The children and I went outside and were standing in the yard. We saw the cars coming. The front one had a cross on the front of it. Every car had the light on in it—you could see everybody, the hoods."

Dino Thompson remembers his mother crying.

"The caravan was coming right through the middle of town," he said in November 2014. "I remember the lead car was a Lincoln Continental. They had welded an angle iron cross to the bumper. It was electrified with red light bulbs, so it was an ominous looking damn thing. We watched it go through town."

At some point while the motorcade was on its way to or in Atlantic Beach, someone in one of the cars learned that Charlie Fitzgerald had called the police and left word that the Klan had better not come back. The cars headed back to Myrtle Beach. An article dated August 30, 1950, in the *Tabor City Tribune* says what followed.

> *Details of a Ku Klux Klan–Negro gun fight in Myrtle Beach Saturday night during which a Conway policeman, wearing a klan robe over his uniform was shot to death, remained sketchy tonight, the Associated Press said Tuesday in an article date-lined in Conway…Killed during the gun fight, which took place in the colored section of Myrtle Beach about midnight, was James Daniel Johnson, 42, who was shot under the left shoulder blade with what is believed to be a .38 caliber pistol. Johnson was carried to the Conway Hospital but died a few minutes after being admitted. It has been impossible to find the names of the persons carrying Johnson to the hospital. Horry County Sheriff C. Ernest Sasser, according to the Associated Press report, said that "300 shots were fired by about 60 robed klansmen and an unknown number of negroes in front of a dance hall and tourist court." Johnson was wearing both his police uniform and a klansman's robe at the time he was shot.*

During the attack, Charlie's Place was shot up and wrecked, inside and out. Charlie Fitzgerald was driven into the country by Ku Klux Klan members, beaten and had his ear cut. Fitzgerald had many more business interests in addition to his nightclub, and one of them was a taxi service. In an incredible coincidence, one of his own taxis drove by where the Klan had dumped Fitzgerald out along SC 544, and the driver picked him up. Not knowing what else to do to protect his boss, the driver took Fitzgerald to the police. He was held in protective police custody in Columbia, and no charges were filed against him in relation to the violence that day.

Other African Americans injured that night by the Ku Klux Klan were thirty-year-old Gene Nichols, who was shot in the foot; Charlie Vance, "about 30," who had internal injuries; and Cynthia "Shag" Harrol, who was "hit in the back several times and required medical attention."

By the time the weekly edition of the *Tabor City Tribune* was published on September 13, a one-paragraph article at the bottom of the front page was headlined "KKK Note."

"The only development regarding the Ku Klux Klan and the Myrtle Beach killing of Dan J. Johnson since last week that has been disclosed is a statement by Circuit Judge G. Duncan Bellinger of Columbia, S.C., in a charge to a jury that the [Myrtle Beach] incident on August 24 [*sic*] was 'a diabolical and outrageous affair.' The judge also said that great responsibility rests upon jurors to discharge their duties and to see that there is an end to mob rule."

The September 20 issue contains the headline "McGrath Brands KKK Communistic; Sasser Investigating." McGrath was U.S. attorney general J. Howard McGrath, and he is paraphrased in the article as saying the KKK "has been on the nation's list of subversive organizations for some time."

"This statement by the attorney general," the article says, "marked the first public notice that the federal government was keeping an eye on the KKK with the idea that it might have foreign allegiance."

The incident also caused a stir at the local level. The article refers to comments made by Horry County sheriff C.E. Sasser indicating he checked up on license plate numbers obtained from vehicles involved in the Charlie's Place attack, but he "found that many of the cars have been sold or traded since taking part in the raid. His investigation has taken him over many western sections of South Carolina and into parts of North Carolina."

An after-effect of the Myrtle Beach KKK attack, the article says, was to inspire other communities to stifle them.

> Since the Myrtle Beach incident, many Klan organizations have folded up and many cities in South Carolina are passing ordinances prohibiting any Klan parades in the future.
>
> The sheriff last week said "It is my honest belief that within a short period the Klan will be extinct so far as Horry County and possibly the

state is concerned. What few men are left in this organization will get out. My information shows that many of the Klansmen who have remained in this order are guilty of many of the misdemeanors that certain unfortunate ones have been punished for by the Klan and therefore, have no right to administer punishment to anyone under any circumstances."

The article wraps up by saying there were plans in motion to "virtually outlaw the Ku Klux Klan" in South Carolina and notes that twelve men in Charlotte, North Carolina, had been recently arrested for "burning crosses in the Charlotte area." Several of them received $200 fines and were sentenced to "six months on the roads, changed to probation pending their good behavior."

Eventually, several Ku Klux Klansmen related to the Charlie's Place incident were arrested: South Carolina Grand Dragon Thomas Hamilton, Conway optician Dr. A.J. Gore, Conway native and Klan secretary-treasurer J.C. Creel, Florence beer truck driver R.L. Sims, Horry County farmer June Cartrette, Bill Bennett, Boyd Ford, Roy Ford, Edwin B. Floyd and Rarien Britt. They were charged with inciting mob violence, and some weren't prosecuted for lack of evidence. The rest had their cases go before a grand jury, which declined to prosecute. Constable T.M. Floyd of Loris lost his job in the aftermath when he admitted he was a Klan member.

No one was charged in the death of police officer and magistrate Dan Johnson. The grand jury and a coroner's jury decided he "met his death by unknown persons."

Charlie Fitzgerald continued to operate his club, but it wasn't the same as before the Ku Klux Klan attack. He was fined seventy-six dollars in September 1950 upon conviction in Columbia of "possession of obscene motion pictures and an unlawful weapon." In May 1951, he was given a choice of a fifty-dollar fine or thirty days in jail for an incident in Charleston when he was convicted of disorderly conduct for "assaulting Dolores Johnson with a knife," according to an article in the *Field*. She was cut on the wrist. And in August 1951, he was convicted in Conway for "selling beer on Sunday and creating a disturbance."

Fitzgerald died of natural causes a few years later. Charlie's Place, a remarkable venue for black soul music and the birthplace of the shag, was gone.

UNABASHED AND UNAPOLOGETIC

While some people may have been optimistic that Klan activities would cease following the Charlie's Place attack, Thomas Hamilton seemed to take the lack of indictments as encouragement. Klan activities increased.

Lillian Mills* always wondered if her husband, whom she later divorced, was one of the Klansmen who shot up Charlie's Place that night in August 1950. She never asked him because she was afraid of the answer. She knew he attended Klan meetings.

> *I went to a meeting with him one night. They had a man up speaking. They had a big cross burning. It was way out in the middle of a field. I don't even know where it was now. It was not in Horry County; it was way away from Horry County. When I left there I was scared, and I never went back again. I just felt like that wasn't for me. I didn't want to be part of it. They just were like no black [person] was worth anything. It was terrible. They were putting them down, and then they did start burning crosses in different places. I probably never told ten people I went there that night with him. But I tell you what, I never went back again. They were rabble-rousers.*

Hamilton pushed a Klan message of American values, virtuous living and anti-Communism in addition to the racist theme. The meeting Mills attended in the early 1950s was likely organized by Hamilton and featured him as a speaker, because he stayed busy in those days crisscrossing the southeast to give speeches and solicit money. The Ku Klux Klan was his profitable business, and speeches that appealed to a broad spectrum of prejudices brought in plenty of new members and income. Mills said the crowd of at least two hundred people at the meeting she attended was mostly couples, "probably as many women as men." She doesn't remember seeing any children there and says she certainly didn't bring her own.

The message at that meeting was all about white Christian supremacy, and it wasn't directed at just African Americans. "A lot of it was Jewish, too," Mills said. "Anybody that wasn't white."

Three months after the KKK attack on Charlie's Place, Hamilton announced a public Ku Klux Klan meeting in Horry County, complete with cross burning.

Horry County sheriff C.E. Sasser said that a week before that KKK demonstration, "a group of Horry County's best citizens came to me and wanted to appeal to the Governor to stop this meeting. I had the law and gave it to them stating, that as long as they had orderly meetings unmasked, there was nothing they could do. I gave an order to all deputy sheriffs forbidding them from attending this meeting. I did have a representative there [without

Standing beside a U.S. flag, Grand Dragon Thomas L. Hamilton of the Association of Carolina Klans addresses a rally attended by five thousand at Conway, South Carolina, on November 11, 1950. *AP photograph.*

authority] and he informed me that the Klansmen that were supposed to direct traffic had guns hung on their side, which was against the law."

Sheriff Sasser also made allegations that six weeks before the demonstration, "when I arrived at my home, one of our best citizens was there waiting. He told me that a certain person at Myrtle Beach was offered a heavy concession to sign a statement that he had paid graft to a law enforcement officer and I immediately called in two deputy sheriffs and another good citizen and went to Myrtle Beach and upon my investigation, found that to be true, not only with him, but others as well."

Horace Carter attended the November 11 demonstration. A cross was burned in a muddy Horry County tobacco field, and thousands of people gathered 'round. His front-page headline on November 15 was "Grand Dragon Charges Lawmen Accept Bribes."

Thomas Hamilton, Grand Dragon of the South Carolina Ku Klux Klan told an estimated crowd of 8,000 people Saturday night in a tobacco field on Highway 917 in Horry County that "the lid will soon blow off in Horry County. I have affidavits showing that some people are having to pay law enforcement officers for the privilege of doing business."

Hamilton, wearing a brilliant silkish green cloak and hood that left his face exposed, was the only speaker on a highly publicized program advertised to disclose what really happened at Myrtle Beach when Conway Policeman Dan Johnson was murdered.

The Myrtle Beach incident, however, was touched only lightly as the Grand Dragon proceeded to blast everything from churches, schools, newspapers and the United Nations to the President of the United States.

Hamilton said that the night Johnson was killed, the Klan was making a peaceful motorcade along public highways with no intention of violence or demonstrations. He said that Charlie Fitzgerald, operator of the café and dance hall where the shooting occurred, dared the Klan to return to his establishment. "And ladies and gentlemen, we being white Americans could not ignore that dare from a Negro," Hamilton said.

THE FLOGGINGS

Hamilton's Klan increased their terrorism after the Charlie's Place violence. Other malcontents who were not Klan members imitated KKK methods to perpetrate violent crimes in the hopes that the Klan would be blamed. Horace Carter continued to report on the floggings and other Klan activities, even though he and his family were threatened with violence and financial repercussions.

Hamilton had a lot to lose if he was forced to shut down his Klan organization. In 1952, the average American annual wage was $3,900. Hamilton had to sell only a couple thousand hoods and robes to earn a decent annual wage, and that was just part of his Klan-related income. He was a Klan mogul.

The Rufus Lee case happened on November 7, 1950. The front door of the white farmer's home was kicked in while he and his two sons, pregnant daughter-in-law and a three-year-old child were sleeping. One of the sons was choked and, according to Sheriff Sasser, "the two boys were marched down the road practically nude (the coldest night of the year) and told: 'If you ever notify the law about this, we will come back and get you. The Sheriff is our next man anyway.' They blindfolded the father, placed him in a car, drove three miles, whipped him, and told him about his drinking and also a message about the law."

On May 2, 1951, Carter reported that, "Stickers bearing the words, 'Yesterday, Today and Forever,' along with 'KKK' were placed on autos, trucks and store windows in Whiteville [North Carolina] over the weekend. These stickers, long familiar decorations on conspicuous windows in Tabor City, had not been noted in Whiteville prior to this weekend."

On Saturday, May 12, 1951, a Klan rally was held near Conway on land owned by Marvin Woodle. About 10:00 p.m. that night, Woodle contacted law enforcement because his home and another nearby home owned by Murphy Graham "had been attacked by gunfire," Carter reported in the *Tribune*. The shooters were Luther Page and his son-in-law, Roy Jackson, who were arrested in Conway on May 13. An Horry County sheriff's badge was found in Page's wallet, so he was also charged with impersonating an officer.

Another nighttime Klan motorcade of thirty-five cars that "roamed up and down several streets and then departed in the direction of Green Sea" was held in Tabor City on Saturday, May 19, 1951. Most of the cars had South Carolina license plates. In June, Carter and Hamilton exchanged barbs, accusations and rhetoric in a letter to the editor and rebuttal.

A Klan rally was held in August 1951 in a dusty cornfield near Tabor City, and the lines of cars "were parked down the road half a mile in both directions," Carter said. In his article about the rally, which he attended, he reported:

Only 97 robed Klansmen were present. At least three were riding horses and had considerable difficulty keeping their steeds quiet while photographers were shooting pictures all over the area. A big cross burned behind the improvised speakers' platform and Klansmen made an effort to march around in a horseshoe figure. However, as some of the daily newspapers pointed out, they were a little rusty on their marching and never exactly got in the swing of the thing. The nearest thing to excitement came when one of the robed Klansmen on the speakers' stand fainted and was carried off by his fellow Klansmen…At least 72 law enforcement officers were at the meeting. Highway patrolmen were kept busy directing traffic.

Carter's articles and editorials gained the attention of regional newspapers and SLED, and then the national media and finally the FBI got involved. FBI agents covertly attended Hamilton's KKK speeches and wrote down the license plate numbers of cars in attendance and then asked SLED and the state highway patrol divisions for South Carolina and surrounding states for help in tracking down who owned those cars. The agency still has long lists of the people who attended those meetings and their addresses.

One of the first journalists outside the Horry County area who covered KKK activities was Charles Kuralt (1934–1997) in Charlotte, North Carolina. Originally from Wilmington, he became one of America's most beloved back-roads storytellers.

"Having the *Charlotte Observer* run my editorial [of July 26, 1950] made me feel a little safe," Carter said in a 2006 interview. "I always felt like if we had some of the big media involved, the Klan would think twice before they did anything to us little boys in the country. Them and the *Raleigh News and Observer* were big helps. And they thought we were helping them by keeping them abreast of what was going on…Charles Kuralt, one of the TV news people in Charlotte, came every Monday to keep up with what happened during the week. He'd make notes, take pictures and go back to Charlotte…and have it that night on TV."

As those early years of the 1950s wore on, many people—black and white—were dragged out of their homes and beaten by Klan members for perceived offences ranging from child neglect and wife beating to alcoholism and gambling. Incidents in 1951 and 1952 marked turning points in the widespread acceptance of KKK activities.

Carter reported one of those occurrences on January 24, 1951. He later said it was pivotal in changing public opinion of the Klan in the southern North Carolina and northern South Carolina areas. The article is headlined

"Columbus Ku Kluxers Not Known," with a subhead of "Several Shots Fired at Fleeing Man."

A mob without robes or hoods but believed to be a band of Ku Klux Klansmen and operating in typical KKK fashion invaded the home of Mrs. Evergreen Flowers, Negro of the Broadway section of Columbus County [North Carolina], two miles west of Chadbourn last Thursday night and administered a severe beating. She was never told the reason for the assault by the mob of "some 40 to 50 men."

Sheriff H. Hugh Nance said this week that there was some reason to believe that the mob was part of the Ku Klux Klan group that has been operating in South Carolina…

The victim, her husband, Willie Flowers, and a ten-year-old daughter were in the house asleep when several cars drove up about 11:30 Thursday night. They awoke and Flowers saw the mob. He said that he then rushed to the back room to get his shotgun but found he had no shells. He claimed that the mob, all white men, then fired several shots when he ran out the back door to go to his brother's house for assistance.

Officers found five empty shells to substantiate this part of the story.

The victim told the officers she was beaten with sticks and a gun and then carried outside to be put in the trunk of a car. She said that one of the mob remarked, "We can't get him. Let's leave her alone."

The young daughter said her mother was hit in the head with a gun. The victim exhibited a gash on her head and bruises on her legs as evidence of the beating.

According to Flowers and his wife, there were eight to ten cars in the caravan. White residents in the section said that they saw the automobiles and said they traveled east to Grice. No one admitted recognizing anyone in the group.

The Klan's typical meting out of "justice," Carter said, involved a man dressed nicely, complete with necktie, who would knock on a person's door in the middle of the night. He'd say his car was out of gas down the road a ways, his wife and children were stranded there and he needed help. Usually the person would agree to render assistance and go get dressed. When they came back to the door, two hooded KKK members would be on the porch, and they'd abduct the person, carry him off in the trunk of a car and take him to a field where several vigilantes beat him up.

Also in January 1951, Carter reported another Klan beating that further enraged local residents. This one took place in Horry County and is headlined "Seven Men Under Arrest in Horry," with a subhead of "Sheriff Sasser Threatens to Summon Troops."

Moving in traditional fashion, a robed band of night riders, said by law enforcement officers of Horry County to be definite Ku Klux Klansmen, beat and rather seriously injured J.C. Gore and his uncle Sam Gore, both of Horry County.

The younger Gore, 25, is a Purple Heart veteran of World War II who has a silver plate in his head from injuries received in battle. He is an 80 percent disabled veteran, who has been treated by Army doctors and psychiatrists.

The elder Gore, 42, a farmer, has been crippled since 1942 as a result of an automobile accident. His beating was severe and medical treatment has been necessary since his flogging.

Taking the same action that was taken following the Myrtle Beach slaying of Klansman Dan Johnston in 1950, Sheriff Ernest Sasser slapped arrest on seven Horry men charged with taking part in the raid. All posted $5,000 bond.

Authorities pressed harder on Hamilton. Sheriff Sasser said "thousands of letters" were confiscated from Grand Dragon Thomas Hamilton's home along with a "10-foot bull whip, two crosses and Klan uniforms." Sasser also reported finding a letter to Hamilton written by Georgia Klan Imperial Wizard Sam W. Roper that read in part, "You have violated every oath and turned traitor to the cause of Klancraft."

As for the men who flogged J.C. Gore and Sam Gore, one of them, D.E. Guyton, made a deal to testify against the other five. Three of them went to trial in March 1951, and they "were found innocent by an Horry County general sessions court" after two hours of deliberation.

A short time later, Sam Gore, one of the flogging victims, was in jail, according to the April 1951 headline "Sam Gore Serves Time for Mistreating Family."

Reports have been verified that Sam Gore who was so publicized recently by being beaten by a robed and hooded gang, is now serving time for the mistreatment of his wife and young children. It was stated by magistrates that Gore's wife came to Conway and took out a warrant for Gore stating that he had beaten her and threatened to kill her and the children, had run them away from home in the cold rain at four o'clock in the morning where they remained until the following day, having been threatened with death if they returned.

Gore, when brought in asked for a jury trial, which he got, and is now serving his time in the Horry County jail.

It was cases such as this that helped the Ku Klux Klan win supporters. In those days before there were battered women shelters, some people looked favorably on the vigilante justice that the Klan dealt out. But others, such as Horace Carter, said there was never a good reason for taking the law into your own hands.

Also in November 1951, two residents in the Tabor City area were awakened around 11:00 p.m. in separate incidents. In both cases, a pair of unmasked men knocked on the door and asked for help with broken-down automobiles. While the homeowners tried to help, masked men pulled up and abducted them. They were carried away to remote spots and beaten "with what seemed to be either a piece of machine belt or a piece cut from an automobile tire." Two men held their arms while they were beaten.

FBI agents jumped on these two Ku Klux Klan cases. One of the victims, Robert Lee Gore (who must have been white because the article does not mention his race), "was carried into South Carolina, and forced to bend over forward while his captors whipped him with heavy instruments," according to a November 21, 1951 article by Horace Carter.

Using Religion

On October 31, 1951, a Klan visit to an Horry County church shocked many people. Horace Carter reported on it in an article dated November 7, 1951:

The parading of 24 robed Ku Klux Klansmen through the aisles of the Cane Branch Baptist Church, near Allsbrook in Horry County, last Wednesday night has again fanned the flames of controversy as both the Klansmen and the arresting deputies face charges.

The big incident began when the parading masked men walked up and down the aisles of the Cane Branch church on Wednesday night during a revival meeting. Sheriff's deputies, having been tipped off to the intended Klan visit, were on hand for the demonstration and arrested 14 members of the parade. Sheriff C.E. Sasser says the arrests were made when the Klansmen stepped back on the public highway. A law was passed during the last session of the S.C. General Assembly making it illegal to wear masks on public property…

All Klansmen were jailed overnight and released on $1,000 bonds Thursday morning.

A letter to the editor about the incident in the November 8, 1951 issue of the *Field* was written by Klan sympathizers and is headlined "The Klan's Visit to Cane Branch Church." It's signed by A.J. Gore, D.B. Spivey and Harvey Johnson.

On October 31, the Klan visited Cane Branch Baptist Church near Loris, S.C. The members were in full regalia while in the church. A considerable sum of money was presented to the minister and appropriate remarks made by one of the Klan members. All was peace and quiet and the congregation seemed to enjoy the visitation thoroughly.

No sooner had the Klan gotten out of the church, walked to the back yard of [the] *same than they were arrested by a bunch of deputy sheriffs. One of these officers carrying a long gun, which could have been an army rifle, came running in rattling the bolt and swinging the barrel in wild grazing sweeps. He is claimed to have said I wish I had a machine gun, I'd mow every one of you down like cutting grass.*

This happened on the church grounds and not on the public road as stated by the sheriff in the News and Courier *on October 31, 1951.*

The constitution of the United States guarantees to the people, the right to "Freedom of Assembly." The grant signed by the seven deacons of Cane Branch Baptist Church gave the Klan the right to visit the church in full regalia. Therefore, the Klan has broken no law, but is completely protected by the law.

Good people of Horry and everywhere, when the time arrives that we are denied the right to freedom of assembly and the other privileges guaranteed by the Constitution then Democracy and freedom will be gone.

Using religion to promote Ku Klux Klan ideals may have been at the foundation of Hamilton's undoing. In early 1952, according to a February 6 article in the *Tabor City Tribune*:

Rev. Eugene Purcell, popular pastor of the Fair Bluff Methodist Church, reportedly was told that it would be unsafe to allow a Negro quartet to sing at a men's fellowship supper. According to the reports he received this message several times. It is also said that the night the quartet was scheduled to sing that several cars bearing South Carolina license plates were parked across the street from the Methodist church and that their occupants remained in them until the Negroes were escorted to their homes without making their scheduled appearance at the fellowship supper. They did not sing.

Alton Bullock, an employee of Scott Motor Company of Fair Bluff and manager of the quartet, said he was approached by a man he did not know who said he was from Florence and told not to let the group sing at the church service.

This incident is reported in the cause of illness of Rev. Purcell at the present time. He is presently on a leave of absence from Fair Bluff. Mrs. Purcell, an expectant mother, it is said was considerably disturbed by the tension and was taken away until the situation has subsided.

Afterward, several ministers of all denominations signed a resolution condemning vigilantes. Hamilton disbanded the Fair Bluff Klavern for "Un-Klanish" acts and wrote in a press release that "some men have joined the Klan there who have taken the wrong attitude and want to take the law in their own hands, and the Klan does not approve of that type activity."

Reverend Purcell never went back to Fair Bluff Methodist Church. Carter reported in February that he "tendered his resignation following advice from his physician that he temporarily retire from his duties. It is understood that he will be inactive in the ministry for some time and is currently residing on his father's farm in the Goldsboro area. He had served as minister of the Cerro Gordo and Fair Bluff Methodist churches for about three years and was among the best-liked young ministers in the state. Fair Bluff residents have expressed considerable regret that his health has suffered to an extent that it is necessary for him to become inactive in the ministry."

"His wife was pregnant, and he was afraid for her," Carter said in 2006. "I guess the Klan thought it would be putting blacks at an advantage if they were in a white church to sing. It's part of the old segregation thing."

BEGINNING OF THE END

About two weeks after Reverend Purcell was intimidated by the Ku Klux Klan, early on Saturday, February 17, 1952, thirty-five FBI agents coordinated visits to several homes. They roused ten men from bed and arrested them on charges of violating civil rights and kidnapping.

The case they were charged for occurred on October 6, 1951, when several Ku Klux Klan members seized Dorothy Dillard Martin and her significant other, Ben Grainger, from Martin's grandmother's home near Fair Bluff, North Carolina. The men took the couple across the state line to Horry County, where they were beaten. "It was reported that the floggers made Grainger remove his clothes and that they beat him until his bowels moved," Carter wrote. The Klan's reasons for beating the pair included "not going to church and possibly immorality."

Taking their victims from North Carolina to South Carolina allowed federal charges to be levied. One of the arrested men, Early L. Brooks, was a former North Carolina police chief, and another was a former policeman. Each of them was released on $5,000 bond.

Ten days later, on February 27, eight more arrests were made. This time the local law enforcement stepped up, and the State Bureau of Investigation and the county sheriff worked together to charge the men

in the case of Esther Lee Floyd, a Negro girl who lives near Chadbourn, on last November 14. The reports of the case are that the floggers drove to the home of her father, drew a gun on him and made him stand still, forced her mother into the bedroom and then abducted the girl. She was not whipped when she told the alleged would-be floggers that she was pregnant but they cut a cross in her hair and told her to "go to Whiteville and tell them the Ku Kluxers got you."

The arrests kept coming. In one case, Carter reported, sixteen men were arrested in Robeson County for simply belonging to the Klan. They were given the choice of "renouncing their memberships and going free, or facing trial under a statute passed in 1868 which forbids membership in a secret political or military organization." Most of them renounced their memberships, which infuriated Thomas Hamilton. His money machine was being ripped apart.

Remorse and Rewards

One of the Klansmen sobbed when he was sentenced for conspiracy, kidnapping and assault for a flogging, Carter reported on May 14, 1952. Ray Kelly of Whiteville received a two-year road term, which was suspended upon payment of a $1,000 fine and one-fourth of court costs.

An outbreak by Ray Kelly's family began as soon as Judge Williams first pronounced his sentence without suspending it, as the pudgy, timid pulp wood worker stood in the courtroom. A grey-haired man several rows back in the courtroom started convulsive movements of his arms and jerking movements of his head. At the same time, he chanted a weird and unintelligible language.

Two highway patrolmen moved to his side and tried to calm him by gently holding his arms. He struggled briefly, then suddenly stopped with an audible, "Hallelujah."

Meantime, Mrs. Ray Kelly broke out in sobs, as did other members of the family. Then she arose from her seat, sobbing, and with a dancing step she made her way inside the bar waving a handkerchief over her head. As she reached her husband, wringing her hands over his head, he, too, began sobbing.

After the sobbing subsided somewhat, Judge Williams ordered everyone to resume their seats.

In 2006, after reading the above article he wrote, Carter commented, "A whole lot of people would have had great difficulty raising $1,000. One thousand dollars, fifty years ago, was a great deal of money. That was high punishment half a century ago."

Finally, on May 28, 1952, Carter got to publish the headline he had been dreaming of for two years: "Klan King Arrested; Conspiracy Charged." Thomas Hamilton was charged with conspiracy to kidnap and conspiracy to assault in relation to two floggings. One of them was the Evergreen Flowers incident, when Flowers "was beaten by a mob 'of 40 or 50 men' and was struck once with the butt of a gun." Hamilton posted the $10,000 bond.

In reporting the proceedings, Carter described how Hamilton fired up prospective members and coaxed them to give him money. "Steve Edmund, the 25-year-old roly poly Columbus farmer who was a star witness for the prosecution in both the state and federal trials, said he filled out his Klan membership blank 'and gave it to Hamilton.' Along with the blank, Edmund said he gave the KKK Grand Dragon $10 as an initiation fee, $6 for a robe and hood, and $2 for the quarter's due."

By the time farmers were again busy sweating in their tobacco fields in July 1952, the Thomas Hamilton chapter of the South Carolina KKK story was over. Some of the Klan members had charges dismissed, and others were never indicted. Others received fines, and a few went to jail.

Thomas Hamilton changed his plea to guilty, and he received the longest prison sentence of all: four years.

In May 1953, Horace Carter's *Tabor City Tribune* and a nearby Whiteville, North Carolina paper where editor Willard Cole also reported Klan activities were the first weekly newspapers to win Pulitzer Prizes.

A few months after the Pulitzer announcement, on October 28, 1953, Carter reported that Thomas Hamilton had publicly renounced his KKK affiliation.

"After he served two or three years," Carter said in 2006, "Willard Cole and I wrote letters to the parole board to say we think he had served long enough. We asked that they let him out on good behavior, and they did. He seemed to me very repentant. He told everyone he regretted his Klan affiliation and would never associate with them again."

By all accounts, that's what happened. Hamilton was released early, and he went home to Leesville and lived a quiet life as a minister. Public Ku Klux Klan activities continued in Horry County under other leadership, with rallies and parades continuing for decades, but the three-year flogging frenzy ceased.

Bibliography

Chapter 1

Dort advertisement. *Automobile Topics* 67, no 5 (September 16, 1922). Digitized on Google Books: 483.

"Fairs Boost Dort Closed Cars." *Automobile Topics* 67, no 5 (September 16, 1922). Digitized on Google Books: 421.

Horry County Historic Resource Survey. New South Associates. Stone Mountain, Georgia, June 30, 2009.

Horry Herald. Advertisement, Sanitary Grocery. September 16, 1920.

———. "Bodies of Five Go To Nichols." August 30, 1923.

———. "Cullipher-Conner [*sic*] Inquest Brings Out All the Facts." September 13, 1923.

———. "Five Cullifers [*sic*], Mrs. M. Conner [*sic*] All Killed by Accident." August 30, 1923.

———. "Mrs. Conner's [*sic*] Body Is Found." September 6, 1923.

———. "Secret Agents Work Tuesday." September 13, 1923.

———. "Taken Under Mortgage." September 13, 1923.

———. "This Dort Was without Brake." September 6, 1923.

———. "What Jury Settled in Recent Inquest." September 27, 1923.

———. "Winston Russ Is Now Clear." September 20, 1923.

Maine Motorist. "Automobile Growth in USA 1922 to 1923." 1924. http://www.machine-history.com/node/373.

Snider, Evelyn. "Glosses on the Maps of Horry County and Conway." *Independent Republic Quarterly* 11 (1977).

Vereen, Ann. Personal interview. Aynor, SC, August 6, 2014.

von Frank, Dr. Julie. Personal interview. Aynor, SC, August 6, 2014.

Walsh, Ellen. Personal interview. Aynor, SC, August 6, 2014.

CHAPTER 2

Atkinson, Susan.* Personal interview. Georgetown County, SC, September 16, 2014.

Bradlee, Ben, Jr. *The Kid: The Immortal Life of Ted Williams*. Boston: Little, Brown and Company, 2013.

Driscoll, Edgar J. "Tom Yawkey, Red Sox Owner, Dies at 73." *Boston Globe*, July 10, 1976.

Georgetown Times. "Mrs. Weisse Dies Monday After Illness." July 23, 1974.

Gutlon, Jerry M. *It Was Never About the Babe: The Red Sox, Racism, Mismanagement, and the Curse of the Bambino*. New York: Skyhorse Publishing, 2009.

Hodges, David Gregg. Personal interview. Pawleys Island, SC, February 7, 2015.

Horry Herald. "Notorious Place Has Been Closed." May 27, 1913.

Huntsinger, Elizabeth Robertson. "Georgetown's Infamous Bordello." *Tidelands*, 2002.

———. *Ghosts of Georgetown*. Winston-Salem, NC: John F. Blair, 1995.

Lee, Alzata. Personal interview. Myrtle Beach, SC, January 16, 2015.

Osteen, Hubert D., Jr. "Nothing Quite Compared to the Sunset Lodge." *Sumter Item*, March 22, 1992.

Pierce, Robert A. "Best Little Shore House in South Carolina." *State*, August 6, 1989.

Sawyer, Paige. Personal interview. Pawleys Island, SC, February 7, 2015.

Williams, June.* Personal interview. Georgetown County, SC, September 16, 2014.

Yawkey Foundation I. Foundation Directory Online. https://fdo.foundationcenter.org/grantmaker-profile?collection=grantmakers&key=YAWK411&page=1&state=%22Massachusetts%22&sort_by=name&sort_order=1&from_search=1.

CHAPTER 3

Field & Herald. "Georgetown Hotel Victim of New Type Swindle." March 1, 1951.

Field. "Myrtle Beach Vacationists Trailed for Dillinger Party." May 24, 1934.

Index-Journal. "Jump Survivor Calls Sport 'Stupid.'" June 9, 1988.

Sun News. "Columbia Girls Found." April 18, 1963.

———. "'Different Kind' of Fourth Crowd Is Area's Largest." July 5, 1962.

———. "Escapee Is Returned to County Jail." September 13, 1962.

———. "Kings Highway Palms Tumble; Two Arrested." October 11, 1962.

———. "Litterbugs Are on Police List." May 3, 1963.

———. "They Have Us Red-Handed, Get Here with Those Fish." July 26, 1952.

CHAPTER 4

Bee. "Drug Arrests Made at Beach." April 3, 1972.

Field & Herald. "Automobile Theft Ring Broken With Arrest of Strickland at Myrtle Beach; 6 Recovered." January 25, 1951.

———. "Thousands Jam Strand Beaches." April 13, 1966.

Gaffney Ledger. "Shop Owners Criticize Treatment of Students." April 3, 1991.

"Horry County Coroner's Office Releases Victims' Names in Myrtle Beach Triple Homicide." WBTW.com, May 25, 2014. http://www.wbtw.com/story/25606823/horry-county-coroners-office-releases-victims-names-in-myrtle-beach-triple-homicide.

Hosking, Bruce. "Myrtle Beach, S.C. Opposes Motorcycle Rallies." Examiner.com, March 31, 2009. http://www.examiner.com/article/myrtle-beach-s-c-opposes-motorcycle-rallies.

Index-Journal. "Beach Arrests Top 1,500." March 29, 1989.

———. "Myrtle Beach Raking in Cash from Increased Patrols." June 13, 1995.

———. "Strand Agents Arrest 120 for Weekend Alcohol Violations." April 4, 1988.

Root, Tonya. "Myrtle Beach Bike Week Attendance Improves, But Still Far Off Old Numbers." *Sun News.* May 22, 2011. http://www.myrtlebeachonline.com/2011/05/22/2172658_bike-week-attendance-rallies-but.html.

Rutherford, Eric. "Myrtle Beach Area's Fall Bike Rally Making a Rally?" *Weekly Surge*, October 16, 2013.

BIBLIOGRAPHY

WMBF News. "Myrtle Beach City Council Passes 15 Ordinances to Limit Bikers." Myrtle Beach, South Carolina, September 9, 2008. http://www.wmbfnews.com/story/8980453/myrtle-beach-city-council-passes-15-ordinances-to-limit-bikers.

CHAPTER 5

Copeland, Larry. "S.C. Alcohol Law Mixes Things Up." *USA Today*, December 29, 2005.

Field. "Moonshiner Falls Prey to Officers While in Well." May 31, 1951.

Florence Morning News. "Big Stumphole Plant Discovered in Horry." February 15, 1956.

Hill, Walter. Personal interview. Conway, SC, November 25, 2014.

Horry Herald. "Bootlegger Is Caught at Game." September 6, 1923.

———. "Get Copper Still." June 30, 1949.

———. "Shows a Disregard Laws and Religion." May 2, 1946.

Item. "Myrtle Beach Approves Sunday Liquor Sales." November 6, 1991.

Lewis, Catherine. "Little River." *Independent Republic Quarterly*, Fall 1990.

Mills, Lillian.* Personal interview. Myrtle Beach, SC, November 20, 2014.

Monroe, Tawny.* Personal interview. Horry County, SC, September 3, 2014.

Sun News. "Search for Radio Produces Liquor." July 4, 1963.

———. "Sunday Beer Sales Begin in S.C." July 21, 2003.

Tabor City Tribune. "Joints Raided, and Still Taken." October 25, 1950.

———. "Liquor Still Captured by Deputy Bell." October 11, 1950.

———. "Vending Machine Hiding Place for Bootlegger." March 4, 1953.

Thompson, Jack. Public speech, Brightwater, Myrtle Beach, December 3, 2014.

White, Chip. Telephone interview. Charlotte, NC, December 3, 2014.

Williams, Richard.* Telephone interview. Columbus County, NC, December 1, 2014.

CHAPTER 6

Howle, Brian M. "Summer of '78: Stoned in Myrtle Beach." *Weekly Surge*, June 19, 2013.

Jenrette, Rita, with Kathleen Maxa. "The Liberation of a Congressional Wife." *Playboy*. Produced by Cohen, Jeff. Photography by Posar, Pompeo. April 1981.

Kingsport Times. "Becomes Floating Museum." June 12, 1978.

Monroe, Tawny.* Personal interview. Horry County, SC, September 3, 2014.

New, Jennifer.* Personal interview. North Myrtle Beach Area Historical Museum, North Myrtle Beach, SC, July 24, 2014.

White, Chip. Telephone interview. Charlotte, NC, December 3, 2014.

Williams, Richard.* Telephone interview. Columbus County, NC, December 1, 2014.

CHAPTER 7

Beacham, Frank. Speech at Myrtle Beach Colored School Museum, Myrtle Beach. November 24, 2014.

Blondin, Alan. "It Was Fast and Furious." *Sun News*, March 19, 2006. http://archive.apsportseditors.org/contest/2006/writing/40-100/40-100_features_first.pdf.

Brown, Roddy. Discussion at Myrtle Beach Colored School Museum, Myrtle Beach. November 24, 2014.

City of Myrtle Beach Comprehensive Plan. Myrtle Beach, March 6, 2014.

Field. "F.B.I. Agents Sieze [*sic*] Gambling Devices at Beach." October 11, 1951.

Hurston, Zora Neale. "Georgia Skin." Florida Folklife from the WPA Collections, 1937–1942. http://lcweb2.loc.gov/diglib/ihas/loc.afc.afcflwpa.3137b1/default.html.

Index-Journal. "S.C. Senate Votes to Keep Video Poker Alive." May 29, 1992.

Monroe, Tawny.* Personal interview. Horry County, SC, September 3, 2014.

Post and Courier. "Video Poker 2.0? South Carolina Sees Spread of New Computer Gaming Machines." July 29, 2012.

Ryan, Jason. *Jack-Pot: High Times, High Seas, and the Sting That Launched the War on Drugs*. Guildford, CT: Lyons Press, 2011.

Smith, Kevin. *Evel Knievel*. the-vu, August 2000. http://www.the-vu.com/2000/08/evel-knievel.

Sun News. "County Police Hit Beach." June 7, 1962.

———. "FBI Arrests Ira Jennings, Boring; Pair Out on Bond." October 31, 1963.

———. "Five Men Plead Guilty in Beach Gambling Case." December 12, 1963.

Thompson, Dino. Discussion at Myrtle Beach Colored School Museum, Myrtle Beach. November 24, 2014.

CHAPTER 8

Field. "Raymond Reinhart, Myrtle Beach Hotel Operator Is Charged with Murder in First Degree in Death [of] Wilmington Atty." April 3, 1952.

Florence Morning News. "Chapman Resigns Horry Police Job." July 14, 1960.

———. "'Ins' Stand Pat on Record; 'Outs' Charge Dictatorial." May 26, 1960.

Gaffney Ledger. "Columbia Man Stuck in Mud, Is Laughed At." July 21, 1928.

Manning Times. "Awful Tragedy." April 5, 1905.

———. "Hung in Horry." October 24, 1906.

Watchman and Southron. "Militia Called Out." October 24, 1906.

CHAPTER 9

Berry, C.B. "Strand Treacherous for Early 'Tourists.'" *Sun News,* April 29, 1995.

Field & Herald. "50 Stolen Swim Suits Recovered by Police." January 12, 1966.

Hill, Walter. Personal interview, Conway, SC, November 25, 2014.

Sun News. "Burglar with Yen for Corn Flakes, Furniture." April 4, 1963.

———. "Looking Back." May 7, 1994.

———. "Patrol, Police, Sheriff Nab Holdup Men within One Hour." August 9, 1962.

———. "Yeggs Made Poor Final Decision." August 9, 1962.

———. "Youths on Escapade." October 18, 1962.

Tabor City Tribune. "Ancient Coin Discovered at Tilghman's Revives Pirate Loot Stories." May 30, 1951.

———. "Cattle Rustling Flourishing Throughout Upper Horry." November 15, 1950.

———. "Mule Steals Bathroom Sink." August 29, 1951.

———. "Southern Granted New Trial." November 1, 1950.

CHAPTER 10

Carter, Horace. "Horry Man Shoots at 'Flying Saucer.'" *Tabor City Tribune*, February 4, 1953.

Collier, Mrs. G.W. "Aynor Schools and Society of the Twenties." *Independent Republic Quarterly* 1, no. 4 (1967).

Dunnagan, Claude. "From the Grand Strand." *Tabor City Tribune*, February 6, 1952.

Horry Herald. "Negro Plays a Trick After He Is Arrested." April 21, 1949.

Mills, Lillian.* Personal interview. Myrtle Beach, SC, November 20, 2014.

Tabor City Tribune. "Mosquito Bomb Gets Dishes Too." August 12, 1953.

———. "Three Youths Held in Theft of Plane." June 18, 1952.

———. "Town Board Warns Air Rifle Owners to Use Caution." February 6, 1952.

CHAPTER 11

Bass, Jack, and Marilyn W. Thompson. *Strom: The Complicated Personal and Political Life of Strom Thurmond*. New York: Public Affairs, 2005.

Baumgardner, F.J., FBI employee, to coworker A.H. Belmont, June 15, 1951. *Klan Activities in the United States Internal Security*. Federal Bureau of Investigation Office memorandum.

Beacham, Frank. Speech at Myrtle Beach Colored School Museum, Myrtle Beach. November 24, 2014.

———. *Whitewash: A Southern Journey Through Music, Mayhem & Murder*. 3rd ed. New York: Beacham Story Studio, 2013.

Brown, Roddy. Discussion at Myrtle Beach Colored School Museum, Myrtle Beach. November 24, 2014.

Campbell, Dr. Walter, and Martin Clark, directors. *The Editor and the Dragon*. Documentary. Narrated by Morgan Freeman. Center for the Study of the American South and Memory Lane Productions, Chapel Hill, NC, April 2013.

Carter, Horace. "Carter's Column." *Tabor City Tribune*, January 16, 1952.

———. "Columbus Ku Kluxers Not Known." *Tabor City Tribune*, January 24, 1951.

———. "KKK Note." *Tabor City Tribune*, September 13, 1950.

———. "Ku Klux Klan Here on Saturday Night." *Tabor City Tribune*, July 26, 1950.

———. "No Excuse for KKK." *Tabor City Tribune*, July 26, 1950.

———. Personal interviews, Tabor City, NC, May–September, 2006.

———. "Seven Men Under Arrest in Horry." *Tabor City Tribune*, January 24, 1951.

Chalmers, David M. *Hooded Americanism: The History of the Ku Klux Klan.* Durham, NC: Duke University Press, 1987.

Epps, Theodosia, ed. *The Independent Republic of Horry, 1670–1970: Items from the* Independent Republic Quarterly. Conway, SC: Horry County Historical Society, 1970.

Field. "Bond Forfeited by Klan Dragon in Floyds Township." May 24, 1951.

———. "Charlie Fitzgerald Arrested, Fined at Myrtle Beach." August 9, 1951.

———. "The Colored People Speak for Their Race." September 6, 1951.

———. "Jury Frees All Five Men of Conspiracy in the Gore Flogging Case Wednesday After Two Hours Deliberation." March 22, 1951.

———. "Klan Dragon Says Meetings to be Held This Week." November 15, 1951.

———. "The Klan's Visit to Cane Branch Church." November 8, 1951.

———. "Ku Klux Klan Holds Rally Near Conway; Two Men Arrested Sunday Charged with Shooting Homes." May 1, 1951.

———. "Sam Gore Serves Time for Mistreating Family." April 12, 1951.

———. "Wampee Churchmen Released as Deputy Bondsmen." November 15, 1951.

Florence Morning News Review. "Governor's Ball and Formal Thanksgiving Opening." Advertisement, Myrtle Beach Sales Company. November 20, 1926.

Hamilton, Thomas. Ku Klux Klan Speech. Sumter, SC. Live speech transcription from files of the South Carolina Law Enforcement Division, Sumter, SC, June 7, 1952.

Hardee, John W. Letter to the editor. *Tabor City Tribune*, August 7, 1950.

Hill, Walter. Personal interview. Conway, SC, November 25, 2014.

Horry County Historic Resource Survey. New South Associates. Stone Mountain, Georgia, June 30, 2009.

Horry County, South Carolina Deed Book C-1 Conveyances 1811–1837, 1849. Abstracted by Catherine H. Lewis. http://www.hchsonline.org/land/deed3.html.

Horry Herald. "Authorities Will Investigate but No Parties Arrested as Yet." September 28, 1922.

———. "Famous 'Birth of a Nation' Will Draw a Big Crowd." August 30, 1923.

———. "Huggins & Rowell Are Cleared in Rape Case." March 17, 1949.

———. "K.K.K. Parade." September 20, 1923.

———. "Rogers Beaten Says a Report." September 20, 1923.

———. "Two White Men Bound Over for High Court." February 17, 1949.

———. "White Supremacy May Be Put to Great Test." April 25, 1946.

James, Veanna. "Infamous History of KKK Recalled." *Tabor City Tribune*, March 19, 1952.

Lewis, Catherine H. *Horry County, South Carolina: 1730–1993*. Columbia: University of South Carolina Press, 1998.

Mills, Lillian.* Personal interview. Myrtle Beach, SC, November 20, 2014.

Ogilvie, J.W. "Horry." *Horry Herald*, September 9, 1901.

Quattlebaum, Paul. "Early Conway as I Knew It." Typed manuscript.

South Carolina Law Enforcement Division. Lists of people who attended Ku Klux Klan rallies, 1950–1953.

Tabor City Tribune. "Governor-Elect Issues Warning as Sasser Replies to Klan Charges." November 22, 1950.

———. "Hamilton Charges." January 23, 1952.

———. "Hamilton Disbands Fair Bluff Klavern for 'Un-Klanish' Acts." January 30, 1952.

———. "Hamilton Renounces All Klan Activities." October 28, 1953.

———. "KKK Stickers on Whiteville Windows." May 2, 1951.

———. "Klan Action Arouses Horry." November 7, 1951.

———. "Klan King Arrested; Conspiracy Charged." May 28, 1952.

———. "Klan Makes Second Trek Down Tabor City Streets." May 23, 1951.

———. "Klan Pays Visit to Mt. Ariel Holiness Church." November 14, 1951.

———. "Klan Shooting Brings Arrests at Conway." May 16, 1951.

———. "Klansman Killed in Horry Gun Fight." August 30, 1950.

———. "Ku Klux Klan Slates Public Meeting, Cross Burning in Horry November 11." November 1, 1950.

———. "Ku Klux Rally Similar to Those Held in Horry." August 22, 1951.

———. "Latest Developments of Klan Incidents." February 27, 1952.

———. "Masked Men Beat-Up Two Columbus County Citizens." November 21, 1951.

———. "McGrath Brands KKK Communistic; Sasser Investigating." September 20, 1950.

———. "Ministers Oppose Floggings." January 30, 1952.

———. "More Mob Action News Is Released." February 6, 1952.

———. "Negro News." November 1, 1950.

———. "Open Meet of K.K.K. Carded Sat." November 8, 1950.

———. "Public Pleased with Arrest of 10 Alleged Ku Klux Klansmen." February 20, 1952.

———. "Robeson Men Face Trial Today on Klan Charges." March 5, 1952.

———. "S.B.I. Arrests Two More for Floggings." April 23, 1952.

———. "S.B.I. Nabs More Klansmen." February 27, 1952.

———. "Six New Defendants Are Named." April 2, 1952.

———. "State Passes Sentence on 11 Night Riders in Johnson Case." May 14, 1952.

Thomas, John. "Slavery in Horry District in the Mid-Nineteenth Century." *Independent Republic Quarterly*, Fall 1982.

Thompson, Dino. Discussion at Myrtle Beach Colored School Museum, Myrtle Beach. November 24, 2014.

Index

ABOUT THE AUTHOR

Reading old newspaper articles is a favorite pastime for journalist Becky Billingsley, and that interest resulted in history from many journalists' perspectives in her first two History Press books, *A Culinary History of Myrtle Beach and the Grand Strand* and *Lost Myrtle Beach*. Now, in *Wicked Myrtle Beach and the Grand Strand*, even more fascinating vintage news sensations are collected in their unvarnished versions. She and her husband, Matt, enjoy bird-watching and visiting historic sites. They live in Socastee and have two adult sons.

Becky Billingsley writes about history and food—often at the same time—in the Myrtle Beach area. *Photograph by Matt Silfer, Silfer Studios.*

Visit us at
www.historypress.net
....
This title is also available as an e-book